"Prograce was the paradigm shift we never knew we needed until we embraced it throughout our ministry and saw how radically it moved us to deeper places of grace and support for women. I have seen it transform our staff, volunteers, and the women we serve, and I believe it is exactly the message the church needs to hear for such a time as this. As the body of Christ, we are called to be agents of healing and grace and to create safe spaces for women to be seen, heard, and supported."

**Tammy Abernethy,** CEO of Hope Women's Center Inc.

"Angela Weszely has given the church a profound gift. In a cultural moment defined by polarizing binaries, she introduces a better way: to be prograce. With theological depth, pastoral insight, and personal authenticity, Angela invites us to reimagine our response to abortion—not as a political stance but as a call to embody the grace of Jesus. This is not just a shift in language; it's a transformation of posture, one that dignifies both women and children and calls the church to reflect the heart of Christ. I'm deeply grateful for this important and timely book."

**Todd A. Wilson,** cofounder of the Center for Pastor Theologians

"With this book, Angela Weszely has brought grace to a topic in desperate need of it. I hope many Christians read and learn from *Becoming ProGrace*."

**Michael Wear,** president and CEO of the Center for Christianity and Public Life and author of *The Spirit of Our Politics*

"*Becoming ProGrace* is a book that every follower of Christ should read. It not only espouses a third perspective on a debate that continues to threaten the unity and witness of the American church, but it also provides a road map to help every Christian engage more thoughtfully and faithfully in the pro-life/ pro-choice debate. In the book, Angela Weszely takes a courageous and bold position, one that invites every believer to reimagine what it means not simply to be pro-life or pro-choice but to be prograce."

**Christy Vines,** executive director of the Center for Peacebuilding and Conflict Transformation at Fuller Theological Seminary

"*Becoming ProGrace* is a bold and provocative contribution to a broader discourse that continues to shape how we think about community, how we perceive our neighbors, and our role in creating a world where all can flourish. Some aspects may unsettle you, and if they do, that's precisely why you need to read it. It raises questions and invites us to examine assumptions we may not realize we hold, including my own. It offers a distinct perspective, one that invites further reflection and opens space for meaningful dialogue."

**Chris Whitford,** CEO of Avail

"'What if we're asking the wrong question?' When I first heard Angela Weszely articulate this question, I found she put words to my angst. For years I had been dissatisfied with the either-or options in the abortion debate, and with her I was finally encountering someone who could articulate not only superior questions but also substantive answers. *Becoming ProGrace* invites readers into the wisdom she's gathered from Scripture, science, diverse friends, and most of all, years of experience. Now is the moment for the church to be equipped to love women and children as Jesus did. *Becoming ProGrace* shows us how."

**Amy Peeler,** Kenneth T. Wessner Chair of Biblical Studies at Wheaton College and author of *Women and the Gender of God* and *Hebrews: Commentary for Christian Formation*

"Drawing from years of experience leading a nonprofit and listening to the stories of women facing unintended pregnancy, Angela Weszely has given Christians today a fresh framework for thinking through abortion. Her prograce approach can help the church learn to better see and love women and children, the image bearers who often get lost amid the well-worn political debates. May this book lead more of us to find a way out of false binaries into the grace and truth modeled by Jesus."

**Katelyn Beaty,** editorial director of Brazos Press and author of *Celebrities for Jesus* and *A Woman's Place*

# Becoming

Expanding the
Abortion
Conversation
Beyond Life
Versus Choice

# ProGrace

## Angela Weszely

ivp

An imprint of InterVarsity Press
Downers Grove, Illinois

**InterVarsity Press**
P.O. Box 1400 | Downers Grove, IL 60515-1426
ivpress.com | email@ivpress.com

InterVarsity Press® is the publishing division of InterVarsity Christian Fellowship/USA®. For more information, visit intervarsity.org.

All Scripture quotations, unless otherwise indicated, are taken from The Holy Bible, New International Version®, NIV®. Copyright © 1973, 1978, 1984, 2011 by Biblica, Inc.™ Used by permission of Zondervan. All rights reserved worldwide. www.zondervan.com. The "NIV" and "New International Version" are trademarks registered in the United States Patent and Trademark Office by Biblica, Inc.™

Scripture quotations marked MSG are taken from The Message, copyright © 1993, 2002, 2018 by Eugene H. Peterson. Used by permission of NavPress. All rights reserved. Represented by Tyndale House Publishers.

*Becoming ProGrace* includes materials adapted from the ProGrace Curriculum and used with permission from ProGrace International. The ProGrace Curriculum is ©2025 ProGrace International. All rights reserved. Any use of this content, including reproduction, modification, distribution or republication, without the prior written consent of ProGrace International, is strictly prohibited.

While any stories in this book are true, some names and identifying information may have been changed to protect the privacy of individuals.

The publisher cannot verify the accuracy or functionality of website URLs used in this book beyond the date of publication.

Cover design: Faceout Studio, Jeff Miller
Interior design: Jeanna Wiggins
Images: © CSA Images via Getty Images

ISBN 978-1-5140-1168-3 (print) | ISBN 978-1-5140-1169-0 (digital)

Printed in the United States of America ♾

**Library of Congress Cataloging-in-Publication Data**
Names: Weszely, Angela, 1968- author
Title: Becoming prograce : expanding the abortion conversation beyond life
  versus choice / Angela Weszely.
Description: Downers Grove, ILL : IVP, [2026] | Includes bibliographical
  references.
Identifiers: LCCN 2025029883 (print) | LCCN 2025029884 (ebook) | ISBN
  9781514011683 paperback | ISBN 9781514011690 ebook
Subjects: LCSH: Abortion–Religious aspects–Christianity
Classification: LCC HQ767.25 .W47 2025 (print) | LCC HQ767.25 (ebook)
LC record available at https://lccn.loc.gov/2025029883
LC ebook record available at https://lccn.loc.gov/2025029884

31  30  29  28  27  26  |  13  12  11  10  9  8  7  6  5  4  3  2  1

This is for Sarabeth and Noah,

for all the ways you've opened my eyes throughout this journey.

With all my love.

*Faith is never the denial of reality.*
*It is belief in a greater reality.*

**BETH MOORE,**
*BELIEVING GOD*


*And so I learned that love is larger*
*than the walls that shut it in.*

**CORRIE TEN BOOM,**
*THE HIDING PLACE*

# Contents

# Preface

# What to Expect

AS AN AVID FICTION READER, I have been guilty of skipping to the end of a novel to make sure it doesn't go somewhere I don't like. So I feel it's only fair that I tell you upfront what you can expect from this book.

The end goal of a prograce response to abortion is that we as the church will become more like Jesus—full stop.

Jesus changed the course of human history, not through political power or any kind of force, but by being a human who acted fully in love. When we reflect Jesus' love and character, his redemptive power works through us to bring positive change in the world. True restoration in society happens not by blaming or trying to control others, but by each of us becoming more like Jesus.

The goal of becoming prograce is not to influence legal access to abortion—or change the thoughts and behavior of others. Rather, it is to look inward and be transformed in the same way Jesus transformed the world—through grace.

It is an opportunity for Christians of all denominations and political affiliations to unite around core values of our faith, such as compassion, kindness, and the inherent worth of every human—values that have been overshadowed by political partisanship and division.

Many conversations over the years have shaped my perspectives. To mirror that journey, I have included some of those conversations in this book, using direct quotes whenever possible. Where I have paraphrased conversations from memory, I've done my best to remove identifying features and protect anonymity. I've used first names or full names only when I've been granted permission to do so.

Each chapter also includes an essay or personal story, written by Christians who represent various denominations and political affiliations, to expand our understanding of what it means to be prograce through diverse perspectives. I'm grateful for every person who has allowed me a window into their experience and shown me through their life what it can look like to live with grace.

I hope you will hear yourself represented in these stories, maybe even in the stories of people you don't expect to relate to because, as fellow believers, we are more alike than we realize.

## BONUS DISCUSSION GUIDE

If you'd like to explore this book with others, go to ProGrace.org/DiscussionGuide to download a free pdf.

# Introduction

# Asking Different Questions

*The reason the [abortion] issue is hard is that you can't accommodate both interests. You have to pick. That's the fundamental problem. And one interest has to prevail over the other.*

SUPREME COURT JUSTICE,
DOBBS VERSUS JACKSON HEARING, 2022

HOW COULD GOD HAVE DESIGNED the creation of human life? Any way he wanted, yet he chose pregnancy. And through that design, God has made it impossible for us to try to help one person while bypassing the other. The woman and the child are intertwined, so that anything we do to one impacts the other. This truth stares us in the face anytime someone is pregnant. Our country's political abortion debate centers around a demand to choose which person we will value or protect over the other—the woman or the child. I know many Christians who feel unsettled by this binary, who believe something about it is off, and yet most conversations I've heard in the church about abortion still revolve around the question "Are you pro-life or pro-choice?"

What if we're asking the wrong question?

Throughout his life, Jesus resisted binary questions that asked him to choose one value at the expense of another. The gospel accounts show this happening almost exclusively with the religious leaders of his society. In many cases, Jesus chose not to provide a direct answer and instead responded with new questions. These questions often prompted the religious leaders and all others listening to look inward and examine the motivations of their own hearts rather than judge others. In the Sermon on the Mount, Jesus asks the crowd, "Why do you look at the speck of sawdust in your brother's eye and pay no attention to the plank in your own eye? How can you say to your brother, 'Let me take the speck out of your eye,' when all the time there is a plank in your own eye?" (Mt 7:3-4).

This is one of the most important questions we can ask ourselves today—no matter what our political and ethical convictions around abortion may be.

In response to the question "Are you pro-life or pro-choice?" I propose alternate questions for Christians to ask:

Is legislation the primary way Jesus brings about change in the world?

Does either political platform (pro-life or pro-choice) offer a full expression of God's redemptive nature?

Does the way we think and talk about abortion accurately represent Jesus?

∾

Jesus taught—and even, more importantly, he showed us through the life he lived—that it is who we are as people that matters most, allowing God's redemptive work to flow through his people and impact culture. As Dallas Willard summarized in *Renovation of the Heart in Daily Practice*, "The revolution of Jesus is one of *character*, which proceeds by *changing people from the inside* through an ongoing personal relationship to God in Christ and to one another. . . . From these [transformed] persons, social structures will naturally be transformed so that 'justice roll[s] down like waters, and righteousness like an ever-flowing stream' (Amos 5:24 NRSV)."

Jesus' emphasis on the priority of our transformed character stands in stark contrast to the US church's collective response to abortion over the past fifty years. In my view, this response has primarily emphasized influencing others—by shaping their moral views, voting behavior, or the legal options available to them. We have been instructed more on how others should believe or behave and less on how we can be transformed by engaging in conversation, listening to people's stories, or learning about the emotional and practical realities that lead to abortion. An approach that prioritizes external outcomes over internal transformation often relies on partisan rhetoric, judgment, or blame to achieve its ends, and it has caused harm in the process. We see evidence of this harm by observing how women relate to the church when considering abortion.

A study from Lifeway Research shows that only 7 percent of all women who have abortions speak with someone at a church before making that decision.[1] It also shows that, while four in ten women are attending church once a month or more at the time of their abortion, the percentage of them who approach a church for help is only marginally higher at 16 percent. Viewing these numbers side by side, we see that even women *within* church communities do not approach the church for support when faced with the decision to carry or terminate a pregnancy. That same study also found that while seven in ten women who have had an abortion identify as Christian, 76 percent of all women say local churches had neither a positive nor negative impact on their decision.[2]

For all our emphasis on outcomes, the church has had very little impact on those who have direct, firsthand experience—known as *lived experience*—of unintended pregnancy or abortion. Worse, we are perceived as unsafe by many women. According to the same Lifeway study of women who have had abortions:

- Women are twice as likely to say they expect a judgmental church response rather than a caring one when facing an unintended pregnancy.

- Women are twice as likely to say they expect a condemning reaction rather than a loving one.

- Sixty-five percent of women say church members judge single women who are pregnant.

Every church leader I've talked with over the years has told me their church wants to be welcoming and supportive for people with this lived experience, and many believe their church would be supportive if someone approached them. What is standing in the way is not our intentions, but deeply rooted mental models we often aren't even aware of. Those perceptions come from our culture as well as the church, and they leak out in our attitudes and words even when we don't realize it. If we're going to be as approachable and compassionate as Jesus was, we have to get to the root of any place these models don't resemble the way Christ valued people.

~

The terms *pro-life* and *pro-choice* don't equip Christians to communicate the inherent worth of both women and children. This is a source of frustration for many people I know who hold complex and multifaceted views on abortion. These labels are political descriptors rather than spiritual ones; they are rooted in specific partisan American politics, and with these terms comes the implicit demand to prioritize one person over the other. The main issue with relying on these partisan terms is that both views fail to convey a comprehensive Christian ethic that recognizes the *imago Dei* (image of God) in all people.

The term *pro-life* emphasizes the value of the child without acknowledging the equal value of the woman, the life-altering impact of pregnancy and parenting, and the societal factors that leave many women and children without essential support. The term *pro-choice* highlights the value of the woman without acknowledging or adequately wrestling with the mystery of God's creation of life through pregnancy, whether at conception or some later stage. These *theological* shortcomings make both terms incomplete in reflecting a truly Christian perspective.

The pro-life/pro-choice binary also makes it very difficult to communicate nuanced *policy* views, such as when or under what conditions abortion should be legal. I know many Christians who support limited legal access to abortion—for example, in cases of rape, incest, life-threatening pregnancy, or during the first trimester or other early stages. This kind of qualified view is their way of communicating that they are considering the needs of the woman more than policies that seek to abolish, criminalize, or prosecute abortion. It also communicates that they are considering the value of the child more than policies that seek to legalize abortion, for any reason, up to forty weeks. But which term can they use to articulate their perspective on legislation?

I have heard Christians who hold complex views say something to the effect of, "I'm personally pro-life but politically pro-choice." While this statement attempts to bridge values from both political parties, relying on partisan labels can make it hard for believers to truly understand each other and find common ground.

In my experience, thoughtful Christians from different political sides have much more in common with each other than with those who lean toward extreme positions on their own side. Over two decades of conversations around abortion, I've encountered very few Christians who appear completely indifferent to the needs of either the woman or the child. Most believers wrestle deeply with these concerns, but the emotional weight and political polarization often keep us from listening well and hearing each other.

For these reasons, I have found it most productive to limit the use of *pro-life* and *pro-choice* in favor of language that helps Christians express a more comprehensive, holistic perspective informed by Scripture and the life of Jesus.

I use the term *prograce* because it elevates the hope of Christ above any attempt to change others through force or argument.

The term *prograce* is grounded in two primary theological pillars applied to the abortion conversation:

1. ***Equal value, equal dignity—honoring the inherent worth in every human.*** If we lead with a political position of pro-life, we will be perceived as valuing the child more, and if we lead with pro-choice, we will be perceived as valuing the woman more—this leads to stereotyping and shuts down conversation with other Christians. If we make our political affiliation secondary to our theological belief in the dignity of all human life, we can honor both the woman and child involved in a pregnancy, which is the fullest expression of God's heart.

2. ***Transformed by grace—relying on the power of grace alone.*** If we become defensive, thinking the problem is the response of other people, we will continue in the same patterns, seeing the same outcomes. If we immerse ourselves in grace, we can look inward to recognize ways we may have unintentionally contributed to division, judgment, and shame in this conversation, instead of creating a culture of compassion in our families, churches, and communities.

Prograce is the posture and language I have found through my journey to best express what I believe: We won't see transformation in society until we, as the church, are transformed by grace. And that belief starts with my own story.

∽

I've never experienced an unintended pregnancy, but I have faced emotional distress around reproduction and motherhood. From high school on, I wanted to go into full-time ministry. I didn't grow up seeing women in vocational ministry roles, but a whole new world opened up to me when I joined campus ministry in college and saw women and men working together with students on campus. I decided to go on staff with an organization right after college, and I felt that my work was equally as important and needed as my male peers' work. I got married a few years later to my husband, Bob, who was also on staff, and I still felt we were treated as equal partners, with similar responsibilities and encouragement from our leaders. And then I got pregnant.

Up until this time, I hadn't noticed that none of the women actively leading discipleship groups had children. When I told my supervisor that I was pregnant and wanted to keep leading one of my groups, she told me she thought I would want to be home full-time once our daughter was born, so she preemptively started to lead my group herself. And that was that. I remember being crushed and angry, but I don't remember pushing back on the decision.

We had our daughter Sarabeth in the summer. When the school year rolled around, our supervisors expected my husband to keep the same schedule he had before she was born, while I was expected to be home with her. I tried to stay involved and brought her along with me to ministry events, but she was 100 percent my responsibility at those events. Sarabeth was active, expressive, and always making sounds, whether happy or sad. I attempted to keep her busy and quiet while also participating in the events, but I felt self-conscious, like I was trying to push something that no one else thought was important.

One day, I casually told a fellow staff member that I was trying to find a way to do ministry part-time on campus, just like my mom had worked part-time when I was growing up. He looked at me deadpan and said, "Well, you just don't value motherhood."

If this happened today, I would have a lot of responses: "Where in Scripture do you find that wanting to work outside the home means not valuing motherhood?" or "You work fifty-plus hours a week on

campus. Do you not value fatherhood?" or even simply "That's ri-
diculous." But I didn't. I said nothing.

This lie entered my heart like an arrow and lodged there, and I
suffered for many years because I believed it. My daughter suffered
because, while she got more of my time, she didn't get the fully alive
version of me. My marriage also suffered because I wasn't being fully
myself. And I grieved the missed opportunity to mentor young
women on campus who I cared about. Worst of all, I had been told
that God was the one behind all of this. I had much respect for
leaders in this organization, because my understanding of God's love
and grace expanded significantly through their teachings and men-
toring relationships. This legacy made the new narrative even more
confusing. My Christian community, where I had found healing, and
where I had received much of my sense of identity and belonging at
the time, was in essence telling me I had to pick between being a
good mother and pursuing my personal dreams; what I wanted didn't
matter, and if I was going to value motherhood, it had to look like
what they told me.

This experience allowed me to begin to understand, even if just a
little bit, what it might be like to face an unintended pregnancy and
feel caught in the narrative that I have to choose between my life—my
dreams, my future, my identity—or my child.

Bob and I eventually left the organization, but I still didn't work
outside the home because of the paradigm I now had around motherhood, even as our finances suffered. When Sarabeth went to school,
and we still didn't have another child due to secondary infertility, I
felt the freedom to work part-time outside the home. After four
years working in some pretty awful sales and substitute teaching
jobs, I took a development role at a Christian pregnancy organization that described their services as providing unconditional
support to women facing unintended pregnancies. I assumed that
meant it was neutral politically. Though I came from a politically
pro-life background, I had always been uncomfortable with the

political rhetoric around abortion and tried to stay away from it. Only after I took the position did I begin to see how partisan, pro-life mental models, messaging, and practices were deeply embedded in the organization.

A year into that role, right as I was going through my last round of infertility treatment, they asked me to interview for the role of executive director. I knew how hard it was to raise a child, and I knew how hard it was to work outside the home with a school-age child. I still doubted whether I could or should try to do both with a baby. I prayed, "God, if I'm going to get pregnant, please let it be before they offer me this role, because I don't know if I can do both."

By the time I completed the interview process, we were past the window of time the doctor had given me to get pregnant, so I took the job. I got pregnant with my son Noah the week I started that new job. Bob knew about my specific prayer, and when we looked together at the positive pregnancy test he said, "Well, it looks like God wants you to do both."

Shortly after I started leading the pregnancy organization, I drove to my hometown of Peoria, Illinois, to attend my twenty-year high school reunion. I was now the face of an organization that was involved in the pro-life/pro-choice debate, and I was nervous about being asked the question everyone would ask me all night long: "So, what do you do now?"

I didn't want to categorize myself or my work into either extreme, so I spent hours crafting an elevator pitch that I felt would be nonpolitical and provide common ground everyone could agree on: "I lead a Christian nonprofit. We serve women facing unplanned pregnancy, and we want to see the number of abortions dramatically reduced." I used that pitch over and over again with dozens of my classmates, expecting a follow-up question like, "Wow, that seems like such a common ground, nonpolitical approach, tell me more." What

I got was silence. Some people even took a perceptible step back from me. Everyone changed the subject.

Time after time, I unintentionally shut down conversations with my former classmates when I told them that I was a Christian who served pregnant women and was concerned about abortion. Even though all three of those were true, the picture they created when I stitched them together was not positive, helpful, or even innocuous. I started to wonder what had been done or said by Christians around the abortion issue that would cause classmates who genuinely liked me to have such a negative reaction, and I decided to look more closely at the practices of my organization.

∾

Our service recipients were women facing unintended pregnancies, and the programs supported our mission of seeing fewer abortions. As I searched our archives and training materials, I couldn't find any materials that showed we had intentionally asked the question of *why* women chose to have abortions. We had built programs around assumptions about the women we served without conducting any meaningful surveys or research to ask them about their experiences.

I found testimonials from women who went to other Christian pregnancy organizations for help, and the pattern I heard when they talked about their experience was very different from the unconditional support and hope I had envisioned when I entered this field. One woman put words to it when she said, "They were only concerned about me giving birth. They treated me like a walking womb."

Hearing women describe their experiences with fellow Christians caused me to examine my own perceptions more closely as well. I said I wanted to support women, but did I understand what that meant? Was my view of helping women informed more by my

Christian values of service and carrying each other's burdens or our country's political rhetoric?

I also asked these questions of the organization I was leading. I knew my colleagues were as well-intentioned as I considered myself to be, so what was causing women to feel unseen? I started to hear my colleagues express a belief that God was primarily calling us to reach out to women within the window of time that they were making a decision about their pregnancy and persuade them not to have an abortion.

My organization and thousands like it were started as outreaches of local churches in the two decades after *Roe v. Wade* was passed in 1973. So my organization was a visible expression of the theology, worldview, and mental model of the Christians from local churches who founded, led, funded, and staffed it. Our practices flowed out of this worldview, and the women we served felt their needs were secondary to our beliefs and our preferred outcome. And my heart broke, because I knew what that felt like.

∽

Many of my beliefs about how God calls Christians to respond to the abortion conversation have been challenged, expanded, and reformed in the past twenty years. I have held unjust stereotypes about people with different political convictions and repented of this judgment once I heard their reasons for that belief and the journey that led them to it. I have gone from a vague sense of understanding why someone may have an abortion to a deep understanding of the barriers, unmet needs, and systemic failures that move people toward that decision. As a result, my paradigm has moved away from believing my primary Christian responsibility is to have the right moral and political view on abortion. I'm now convinced that my primary responsibility is to be inwardly formed in the image of

Jesus and allow his love to overflow into my family, church, work-place, and community.

What hasn't shifted significantly for me is how I view the practice of abortion itself. I believe God takes an active role in creating every human life, meaning abortion is an unnatural interruption of his creation. Through both conversations and research, I've come to understand this interruption impacts every person in-volved. I have not talked to a single woman or man who *wants* to experience an abortion or who does so without seriously consider-ing and wrestling with the complexities involved.

My political convictions about abortion today don't fit neatly on either side of the political spectrum. I have a deep reverence for God's involvement in human life that remains unshaken, and I am passionate about advocating for policies that provide support to pregnant women, such as accessible and affordable healthcare and childcare, flexible work environments, protection from pregnancy discrimination, and paid maternal leave.

The ProGrace community is made up of thoughtful Christians who fall across the spectrum of political beliefs, which means I work every day with Christians who fall to the right and the left of me. Regardless of our different perspectives, we unite around shared values, offer grace to each other in our conversation, and collaborate to pursue change. We are united by our fierce commitment to honor the *imago Dei* in every person and work for justice through the trans-formative power of grace.

The church of Jesus is one-of-a-kind in our country and world. When truly walking in Jesus' ways, the church can offer more hope, belonging, and unconditional support than any other institution in our society. At the same time, when we don't walk in his ways, we have the potential to cause more harm than other institutions, spe-cifically because we are claiming to represent God.

With every election cycle and shift in abortion legislation, I'm en-couraged to find an increasing number of Christians who feel tension around the political divide and are actively seeking a framework that more fully represents Jesus and honors the *imago Dei*. Being prograce means understanding that the church can be a redemptive force in the world when, and only when, we are people who collectively resemble Christ. This, unlike the talking points of our political parties, is a uniquely Christian response to abortion.

# PART 1

# The ProGrace Framework

# 1

# Equal Value, Equal Dignity

*For you created my inmost being;*
*you knit me together in my mother's womb.*
*I praise you because I am fearfully and wonderfully made;*
*your works are wonderful,*
*I know that full well.*
*My frame was not hidden from you*
*when I was made in the secret place,*
*when I was woven together in the depths of the earth.*
*Your eyes saw my unformed body;*
*all the days ordained for me were written in your book*
*before one of them came to be.*

PSALM 139:13-16

PSALM 139 BEAUTIFULLY DESCRIBES God's intentionality in creating, valuing, and sustaining life, and it's a passage I have always
loved. Growing up, I remember my Sunday school teachers reading
this verse to us and using it to describe God's view on the child involved in an abortion. I didn't hear it applied to the woman who was
pregnant. But about a year or so into leading the pregnancy organization, I remember walking through the office hallway one day, when
I suddenly felt this impression in my spirit: "You know that passage
in Psalm 139? It's just as much about the woman."

I never intentionally de-emphasized the woman in my work, and
I don't believe my colleagues did either. At the same time, the

language we used, especially with donors, almost exclusively emphasized the value of the child, playing into the binary that we must
choose one over the other. I felt grief realizing I had unknowingly
contributed to the harmful views of women and motherhood that
had also wounded me. Finally I could put it into words: I wanted to
find a way to be for *both* the woman and the child. The relief I felt in
saying this was not just professional, it was personal.

I started looking more closely at practices in our organization,
and I found we gave information more often than we asked questions to seek greater understanding of the people we served. Our
staff routinely showed models of fetal development, gave pamphlets
on parenting and adoption during the first visit, and shared their
moral views on abortion without being asked. I also learned that
some of the information we gave out, specifically around the risks
and procedures of abortion, was not from neutral, trusted medical
sources but instead overstated the physical and mental health risks
without substantiated evidence. I asked questions of other leaders
from other pregnancy organizations and found some of them shared
similar practices.

I wanted to hear and understand perceptions from people on both
sides of the debate, so I asked friends and neighbors about their
views on abortion without disclosing mine. As I prioritized listening
over sharing, I started to hear the specific concerns people outside
my faith community had about Christian outreach to pregnant
women. The most common concern I heard was that we would try
to persuade or manipulate women regarding their pregnancy decision and religious beliefs.

When I tried to network with local health centers, asking if they
would refer pregnant women to our organization, I would eventually
get asked, "Do you try to persuade women not to have an abortion?
Do you proselytize?" We advertised ourselves as providing unbiased
pregnancy help and counseling. I could empathize with the fear
someone would feel if they came expecting non-biased pregnancy

help and instead received advice about what decision to make; I had never received advice about similar life decisions from a physician or mental health professional.

Holding these concerns up to the ministry of Jesus, I became convinced we weren't seeing or hearing women nearly enough, and I felt responsible for changing this. With our board's full support, I worked with several key staff members to reform these practices, and any others that were not empowering to women or reflective of Jesus' ministry. We trained our team in theology, active listening, and social work practice. We made these changes by 2008, based on convictions of our faith, well ahead of legislation to regulate faith-based pregnancy organizations that began to be introduced at the state level in the years that followed.

I remember not fully understanding where my passion came from, since I had no personal experience with unintended pregnancy or abortion, but I know now. In the deepest parts of me that I didn't fully understand, I was grieving for women who experienced hurt from Christians as a part of the grief I felt for myself.

## RECONCILING OUR EXPERIENCES

Two vivid memories from my upbringing continually came to mind when as an adult I sought to address abortion, and I knew I had to process them before I could bring any change to the organization.

The first memory is from when I was a freshman in high school. I remember sitting in a circle in my friend's bedroom with several other girls. It was a typical 1980s teenager bedroom, with posters on the wall and a floral bedspread. I don't remember exactly how it came up, but my friend told us she had gotten pregnant and then had an abortion. She smiled as she told us, "But there's nothing to worry about, because the doctor told me it was just a blob of tissue." I remember thinking it was odd that she was smiling through what seemed like a very painful and grown-up experience, and I wondered if she needed anything from us at that moment. But I could barely digest what she was saying because I hadn't even kissed a boy, so I don't remember saying anything at all.

The second memory was a few years later, the summer after my sophomore year in college, when an older Christian I trusted encouraged me to attend a peaceful march for life. I believed it was my Christian duty to participate in the march, so I went. When I arrived at the start of the march, they asked me if I wanted to carry a sign and I declined. We walked through the streets of my hometown, ending at a rally in downtown Peoria, Illinois. I couldn't shake the anxiety and shame I felt wondering how my friend from high school, who had confided in me about her abortion, would feel if she saw me walking with that group. What I didn't know at the time was that our march would have done absolutely nothing to support or help my friend when she was facing an unintended pregnancy. On some level, I knew it wasn't what she needed. But I didn't actually *know* what she needed, so I vowed to never participate in a protest like that again, and I largely avoided engagement with the abortion issue for nearly two decades.

Once I faced the shame I felt about these past experiences around abortion and realized how this connected to my own experience, I was better able to process the concerns I had about my organization with compassion and grace. I knew there was a different pathway forward if we could lean in more to God, specifically in the areas where we were operating with only half of the truth.

## DANGEROUS HALF-TRUTHS

The Bible is the Word of God. And yet we see precedence in Scripture that it can be twisted. For example, Satan subtly misquotes Scripture to Eve in Genesis 3:1-3: "Did God really say, 'You must not eat from any tree in the garden?'" When God's actual words in Genesis 2:16-17 were, "You are free to eat from any tree in the garden, but you must not eat from the tree of the knowledge of good and evil." Also, when Christ is tempted in the wilderness in Matthew 4:1-11 and Luke 4:1-13,

Satan quotes Psalm 91 accurately but misapplies it to try to get Jesus to turn against God; Jesus refutes him with Scripture.

We have an enemy who wants to steal, kill, and destroy. These examples show us that one of his tactics is to misuse and twist Scripture until it no longer represents God's true nature. This tactic of Satan can appear in some Christian teachings on abortion that use Scripture to promote half-truths: Either that God is more concerned with the child but not the woman, or that he values the woman but not the child.

This is largely because both political camps in our country's abortion debate use half-truths as part of their rhetoric. But our Christian beliefs are grounded in a much more comprehensive story about who God is and what he values, so our theological teachings about abortion should not fit neatly into either political camp. God creates, cherishes, and sustains all life. He has created our world to be interdependent, meaning whatever we do to one part of creation will impact the whole of creation. We see this perhaps most viscerally in pregnancy.

Understanding the whole truth of passages like Psalm 139 can be equally challenging for Christians who identify as pro-life or pro-choice. There is a deep mystery to exactly how and when God uniquely knits together each person, and we are all responsible for wrestling with that mystery when thinking and talking about abortion.

We live in an age with so much medical advancement that it's easy to think we have control over our bodies. But pregnancy is an intensely vulnerable and unpredictable reminder that we do not. It's vulnerable because there is no other time in our lives when we are so interdependent with another person. Perhaps God chose this way of bringing life into the world to serve as a constant reminder that he created us to be interdependent with each other and with creation.

## ETHICAL CONVICTIONS
Broadening our paradigm around abortion to communicate God's equal value for the woman and the child does not pose a threat to

the ethical convictions we hold; it actually strengthens them. I consistently see that when we follow Jesus' example to look inward and ask different questions, we don't become less concerned about what we were passionate about before. Instead, God expands our concern to encompass *more*. He is more concerned about injustice than we are, not less. He is more concerned for the life, the dignity, and the welfare of the woman and the child than the most vocal pro-life or pro-choice advocates.

We see this as a consistent pattern in the life of Christ. He was constantly confounding and infuriating the religious leaders, and sometimes even his disciples, by elevating God's value for all humans.

- The woman with the issue of blood was not supposed to be near Jesus or touch him because she was considered unclean and a social outcast. She was trembling with fear when he asked her to come forward, but Jesus called her "daughter" and blessed her with peace (Luke 8:43-48).

- Jesus called Matthew, who was hated and considered a sinner and traitor by his people because he collected taxes from them for the Romans, to be one of his twelve disciples. Then Matthew gave a banquet at his home for Jesus and invited many more tax collectors. The religious leaders grumbled to Jesus' disciples that he shouldn't be attending feasts with sinners like them (Luke 5:27-32).

- The religious leaders interrogated and criticized Jesus for wanting to heal a man on the Sabbath, a day on which the Hebrew law didn't allow people to work. Jesus asked if there was any one of them who wouldn't rescue one of their sheep who had fallen in a pit on the Sabbath. He went on to heal the man, saying that it was lawful to heal on the Sabbath because a person is so valuable to God (Matthew 12:9-14).

John 3:16, the most quoted verse in the Bible, tells us that God's profound love for each and every person in the world was the entire reason he sent Jesus to us. The New English Translation Study Bible says that in using the phrase *God so loved the world*, John is in effect saying, "God loved the world in this way." He is emphasizing "both the degree to which God loved the world as well as the manner in which he chose to express that love. This is in keeping with John's style of using double entendre or double meaning. Thus, the focus of the Greek construction here is on the nature of God's love, addressing its mode [sending Jesus], intensity, and extent."

## THE KINGDOM OF GOD IS LOVE

My family and I started attending the Vineyard Church in Oak Park, Illinois, when Sarabeth was in elementary school. Bob and I knew from the moment we walked in the door that we were home, even though we couldn't articulate why. The lead pastor was named Dave, and his wife, Anita, was copastor. This was the first time I had been a part of a church with a woman at that level of leadership. Even more interesting was Dave's theological conviction at the time that, based on Scripture, women aren't to be the lead pastor of a church—but that is the only thing they can't do. I watched Anita and Dave both encourage and challenge women, regardless of how many children they had, to step into roles of influence and leadership, including myself. I was leading worship and serving on the church council when I got pregnant with Noah, and I was so surprised when no one questioned if I wanted to return after he was born. They wanted to know *when* I wanted to return, not if.

My community at Vineyard helped heal me from the lie that I had to choose between parenting and ministry because of my gender. It was also the first practical expression I saw of the Vineyard's understanding of the kingdom of God. Their core beliefs state: "Since the kingdom of God is the future reign of God breaking into the present through the life and ministry of Jesus, we are a forward-leaning movement emphasizing the ever-reforming nature of the church engaging the world in love."

We spent a lot of time studying Jesus—his life, relationships, teachings, and parables—in a way I had never experienced before, and then I witnessed it actually being lived out. We empathized with people's suffering and boldly prayed that God would heal and comfort them. We also engaged in practical acts of service and generosity that would alleviate people's suffering. Expressing God's love and goodness to each other and our community was more important than political or even theological differences. We still talked about those things, searched the Scriptures to discern truth, and held strong convictions, but we always came back to Jesus as our model for how God engages with us and wants us to engage with each other. The Vineyard is where I developed a passion for having a kingdom-of-God allegiance above any other allegiances (including political allegiance). It's also where I learned, through experience, that all people really do have equal worth, dignity, and value in the kingdom of God.

Dallas Willard says in *The Scandal of the Kingdom*,

> When we speak of the kingdom of God, we are speaking of a kingdom which works more like a family or a well-functioning neighborhood, where people really do *love* one another and care for each other. This kingdom is the range of God's effective will—or simply God acting in this world—where what he wants done is done. Jesus' teaching showed us that the kingdom of God is not a thing of times and places; it is a thing of the heart. It is a life that is lived in vital connection with God himself. Unlike the kingdom of God, human government functions on principles of force, deception, brutality, and the power of death. All human governments have the power of death, but what they lack is the power of *life*. This is what the kingdom of God has: *the power of life.*

Eventually I connected the dots that if all people have equal worth, dignity, and value in the kingdom of God, then the church desperately needed new ways of thinking and talking about abortion.

## WE MUST LOOK INSIDE

I am asking Christians to conduct an honest evaluation of our response to abortion by holding ourselves up to the example of Jesus and asking if we are grounded in God's passionate commitment to each human. I am not claiming this will give us all the outcomes we hope for in what will continue to be a complex moral, political, and social issue. Uniting around a commitment to the equal value of every person won't solve every challenge when a woman's agency seems to be at odds with a child's well-being. But a firm commitment to the *imago Dei* in every person must be our highest value and plumb line.

In a political dialogue where even the most beautiful theological language has been weaponized, it's critical to focus on our own character and meditate on God's love for every person. Perhaps the best place to start is with the people we disagree with, don't understand, or have previously considered "the problem." Once we are grounded in this value, Christians will be more able to unite across differences in pursuit of the kingdom of God, opening up new pathways for true and lasting change.

### The Incarnation Affirms Equal Worth
#### —Rev. Dr. Amy Peeler

The idea that God is our Father and we are children of God can feel like a given for Christians today, but it's pretty radical. At the same time, much of that family language is gendered masculine, as Father and Son. For a long time, I wondered where women fit in this story of God's family.

Navigating the world of theology as a woman and a professor, I interact almost daily with young female students who, sometimes kind of lightly and sometimes in tears, ask this same question: "Do I belong in Christianity? This faith seems like it's for the guys. Where do I fit?"

As my research progressed through multiple years, our country and the church became more divided on various issues. On the issue of unintended pregnancies and abortions, the lines were so stark, and I found myself frustrated. I didn't want to belong to either extreme. I was doing exegetical work with the story of Mary, the mother of Jesus, a woman at the center of the Christian story, and the Lord gave me new insights that address that frustration.

Mary was in a very precarious situation. When Gabriel comes to her, all he says is, "You will bear a son. He will reign forever on the throne of his father, David." Gabriel does not say, "You're going to be fine. You're going to make it through this." He doesn't mention Joseph at all.

The conception happened before Joseph received his angelic vision, and Mary had no guarantee that he would protect her and take her into his home. So she said yes, knowing the potential costs and the potential abandonment by him.

Of course, Christians should be compassionate to women facing unintended pregnancy, but not just in a general way. We should be compassionate because this is the story we follow—this is our Lord's story.

God could have saved us in any way, but he chose incarnation. Now every time a baby is born, we're reminded that he designed human biology so that God could dwell among us and take on flesh. And when God made that decision, Mary was necessary. What clicked for me in a deep and transformative way is that any stance I take on this very complex topic must be motivated by compassion for the lives of both. Theologically, this has been radical.

The second feature of Mary's story that truly transformed my thinking is how God respects her agency. When Gabriel comes, he says, "You will have a son." But notice that it is in the future tense. It hasn't happened yet. He didn't say, "You are already pregnant."

In her conversation with Gabriel, she's perplexed and disturbed. She asks a question, which allows him to tell her this is not a messiah like she might have imagined. "Your child will be holy and called the Son of God. Nothing is impossible with God." The narrative could have ended there, that nothing is impossible if God can make a virgin into a mother. But Luke tells us that Gabriel waits to hear what she says. He departs only after her spoken consent.

I very intentionally use the word *consent*. I do that as a biblical scholar because in the ancient world there were many stories of gods who raped women. So, writing in the first century, it was important for Luke to disassociate the incarnation from those stories. He needed to show that God was not transgressing or using Mary but that she consented. I found such beautiful resources about this truth in all trajectories of Christian tradition, from Catholics to Orthodox and all types of Protestants. Nobody disagrees that Mary gave consent; it is not forced on her. So we all agree. And that's a rich thing to celebrate and to motivate us toward unity in a conversation that nonreligious spaces are still deeply confused about. Christianity has something incredibly positive to offer here. In God's good providence, we have some profound truths that can translate to several complicated issues.

Last, I did more work in understanding all of the biblical language and imagery for God, which seems to be oriented very much toward the male side of an equation. So if we go back to basics, we know God is God. God is not a creation. God is the Creator. Jesus tells us in his conversation with the Samaritan woman that God is spirit. God is not embodied until Jesus does the gracious act of taking on flesh.

Genesis 1:27 tells us God created both males and females in his image. That passage not only tells us about humans, it tells us something about God: God is not more or less one or the other. God encompasses all of the qualities that we describe as masculine or feminine. So why does Scripture give us the language of the Father?

I call God my Father because Jesus did. Why did Jesus call God his father and not his mother? Because he already had a mother—Mary. For most of my adult life, I've been asking where women fit into church. Mary, giving of her flesh so that God could become incarnate, says, "Women, you're a part of this story." Jesus, in his maleness, says, "Men, you're a part of this story." Nobody's left out. That's how God works.

---

*Rev. Dr. Amy Peeler is a New Testament professor at Wheaton College, an ordained Episcopal priest, and the author of* Women and the Gender of God.

# 2

# Transformed by Grace

So what does it mean to live with grace in the context of the abortion debate? At the beginning of his Gospel, John begins to explain the centrality of grace in Jesus' identity:

> The Word became flesh and made his dwelling among us. We have seen his glory, the glory of the one and only Son, who came from the Father, full of grace and truth. . . . Out of his fullness we have all received grace in place of grace already given. For the law was given through Moses; grace and truth came through Jesus Christ. (John 1:14, 16-17)

The Greek word for "grace" in these verses is *charis*, and it means favor, kindness, blessing, gift—all with the connotation of being unearned. This word occurs 157 times in the New Testament and is one of the primary foundations for how we are formed to be more like Christ. According to the Strong's Commentary Lexicon from the *Discovery Bible*, "In the Greco-Roman world, 'charis' was commonly understood as a favor or gift given without expectation of return, often to cement social bonds or express goodwill. In the New Testament, this concept is deepened and transformed to express the profound and unconditional love of God toward humanity, which is not based on human merit but on God's own character and purpose."

The concept of *grace*, however, originates in the Hebrew Bible. It's rooted in the word *khen*, which means grace, favor, merciful, and compassionate. According to the Bible Project, God's grace is "his free gift of life and goodness, rooted in enduring love for humanity. It reflects his nature to love without end, providing generously without regard to merit."

## UNDERSTANDING GRACE

When I first started this work, my instinct was to prioritize extending grace to someone who had experienced abortion, without recognizing my need for grace in how I thought or spoke about the topic. Now, when I talk about living with grace in this context, I am primarily talking about the grace I need to engage like Christ. This is often the most challenging part—admitting that I haven't always valued both the woman and child equally, and accepting God's grace for my role in this.

I didn't begin to process my own uncomfortable experiences around abortion until I had a deeper understanding of grace, since it involved admitting I had caused other women pain by failing to consider their reality. I had a tendency to experience shame any time I thought my behavior was off the mark, and so I tended to deflect that shame by trying to blame others.

Recognizing I need grace is recognizing I'm human. Recognizing others need grace is recognizing they are also human. Grace is an understanding of the human condition. We all make decisions out of survival. We all are in places of need and use different means to try to get what we need. We don't rank those decisions, some as better and some as worse, because that isn't how God operates when he extends forgiveness.

Once we understand this for ourselves, we can offer grace to fellow believers who are also wrestling with their views and actions. We'll need a lot of grace for each other as we seek a non-political, kingdom-rooted approach, finding theological common ground rather than letting politics define the conversation. Only after we've done this internal and communal work can we authentically embody grace toward those with lived experience.

## GRACE OVER SHAME

I have been deeply impacted over the past ten years by the research of Brené Brown, specifically her findings that shame is not effective for changing human behavior. Shame prompts us to have negative thoughts and feelings toward ourselves, but it does not empower or motivate us toward change. In fact, it moves us toward more harmful behavior.[1] I see a direct correlation between Dr. Brown's findings and the narrative of Scripture. We experience transformation by knowing our worth, and for Christians, the story of our worth begins at creation.

Genesis says God saw that everything he made was very good (Genesis 1:31). The Hebrew word for "good" here is *tov*, which means excellent, rich, and valuable. But we get a much clearer picture with the Hebrew word for "very" which is *meod*, meaning exceedingly, abundance, force, might. This verse tells us that everything God creates is *exceedingly good*. Then he goes further and makes humans in his image, his very likeness, the *imago Dei* (Genesis 1:27). We see the story of God bestowing worth on humans and pursuing us throughout the Scriptures, and then we come to the gospel—the good news—of grace.

If we believe in the entire story of Scripture, including the love that initiated the gift of grace, then we also believe in our inherent worth as humans. When that belief is secure, we no longer have to fear challenging conversations with others who disagree with us. We can let our guard down and recognize that same inherent worth in them. Extending grace to those who disagree with us keeps us from sliding toward the dehumanization that has begun to characterize so much of our public discourse on divisive topics.

Grace also helps us step back and consider our attitudes and language toward people with lived experience. Our cultural narrative around unintended pregnancy tells the woman that she is a different person once this has happened to her, that her identity has changed. Have you ever heard any of these things said?

It's too bad, because she was such a smart girl.

How could she have let this happen?

It's like she threw her future and her life away.

These messages reinforce a narrative of shame, damaging a woman's sense of self, alienating her from her faith community, and sending the message that a woman must choose between herself and her child.

Grace, however, communicates a message that can repair that harm.

Her identity remains unchanged; she is the same person she has always been.

We all walk through times of struggle, and there is always hope.

God has compassion on all of our struggles, without ranking or categorizing them.

The culture within our families and faith communities can change significantly when our attitudes and words reflect an understanding of our shared struggles and the expansiveness of grace. When we are truly committed to recognizing the *imago Dei* and grace of God for each person, we are effectively communicating that we will not view those who experience unintended pregnancy or abortion as defined by that for the rest of their lives. This grace has the power to undo narratives of shame that have been around for centuries. It reminds us we are together, as Christians, and as humans.

Growing up, I tried really hard to be what I believed a good Christian was, and I believed that my ability to be close to God was dependent on how well I did. I subconsciously ranked myself with other people by judging their behavior, because that could allow me to feel I wasn't so bad. When I understood that God accepted me exactly as I am, it changed the way I looked at everybody else.

When we dig in our heels to defend what we think it means to be a Christian, often in opposition to other people, we betray the life of freedom under grace that God intends for us. I am convinced that the reason it is so difficult to apply the principles of grace to contentious societal issues is because we do not understand grace for ourselves.

## THE CHRONOLOGICAL ORDER OF GRACE

To begin to understand what that life of grace looks like, we look to the example of Jesus in John 8.

> At dawn [Jesus] appeared again in the temple courts, where all the people gathered around him, and he sat down to teach them. The teachers of the law and the Pharisees brought in a woman caught in adultery. They made her stand before the group and said to Jesus, "Teacher, this woman was caught in the act of adultery. In the Law Moses commanded us to stone such women. Now what do you say?" They were using this question as a trap, in order to have a basis for accusing him.
>
> But Jesus bent down and started to write on the ground with his finger. When they kept on questioning him, he straightened up and said to them, "Let any one of you who is without sin be the first to throw a stone at her." Again he stooped down and wrote on the ground.
>
> At this, those who heard began to go away one at a time, the older ones first, until only Jesus was left, with the woman still standing there. Jesus straightened up and asked her, "Woman, where are they? Has no one condemned you?"
>
> "No one, sir," she said.
>
> "Then neither do I condemn you," Jesus declared. "Go now and leave your life of sin." (John 8:2-11)

When I read this passage, I try to imagine this scene as if I were there. I feel a sense of much-needed peace and anticipation as Jesus sits down to speak. I'm taking a few deep breaths, settling in for the refreshing experience I've come to know and love from Jesus, when all of a sudden, there is a massive disruption. I have to stand up again to see what is happening, and I'm shocked as a group of religious teachers, some of whom I've known since childhood, forcefully place a woman in bedclothes in front of Jesus. I feel compassion for her and want to help cover her up. And yet these teachers are my spiritual authority, and they are the ones initiating this. I can feel anxiety and confusion rising up as I wait to see what Jesus will do.

As I imagine the anxiety of this moment, one of the primary things that jumps out from this story is the chronological order of how Jesus responds.

**First, Jesus defuses the situation.** Right away, he defuses the situation by refusing to address what the religious leaders ask him. Scripture tells us the Pharisees set up this situation to trap Jesus. They waited until he was in front of a large crowd, right in the temple, and they must have thought they had him when they said, "In the Law, Moses commanded us to stone such women. Now, what do you say?" (John 8:5).

If he said "Don't stone her," they could say he was disregarding God's law and could point out the inconsistency of the statement he made earlier in Matthew 5:17, "Do not think that I came to abolish the Law or the Prophets; I did not come to abolish them, but to fulfill them." They could discredit his ministry and his claim to be the Messiah.

If he said "Stone her," the people would be horrified that the gentle teacher had acted unmercifully, instead promoting violence, and many would stop following him. He could also have become a target of Roman legal action. (In John 18:31, the religious leaders tell Pilate they have no right to execute anyone without Roman authority or permission). Jesus doesn't fall into their trap, partly because his first response is to ignore what the Pharisees asked him.

When I imagine this scene, I picture the religious leaders angrily pushing the woman to stand before the crowd, and heatedly asking Jesus to make a judgment on the woman's behavior, on her guilt. I love the understated way the Scripture says, "But Jesus bent down and started to write on the ground with his finger." He didn't answer. He didn't get defensive or panicked. He didn't say anything at all.

We don't know what he wrote on the ground. Saint Augustine thought he wrote with his finger to represent that the same finger that wrote on the tablets of Moses was in their midst. Jesus was the author of the very law they were trying to quote to him. Many scholars, including Saint Jerome, think Jesus' reason for writing in the dust is linked to Jeremiah 17:13: "Those who turn away from you will be written in the dust because they have forsaken the LORD, the spring of living water." They believe that by acting out this Scripture, Jesus was pointing to the fact that the religious leaders' hearts were hardened toward God, not trying to uphold his law as they claimed.[2] Whatever the reason for Jesus writing in the dirt, I can imagine it confused the crowd. I imagine people craning to see what was happening, surprised that he wasn't responding to what the Pharisees asked him.

The Pharisees kept questioning him, so he straightened up and spoke wisdom, grace, and life into the situation. And then again he stooped down and wrote on the ground. John says he remained stooped as the accusers began to go away one at a time. Jesus only straightened up when they were all gone.

Why did Jesus physically stoop down? Was it simply practical, so he could reach the dust? Or was it a symbolic act? Again, we don't know, but it's worth noting that the Greek word for "stooped down" only appears in one other place in the New Testament, when John the Baptist says he is not worthy to "stoop down" and unlace Jesus' shoes (Mark 1:7). The only other picture we see of God stooping down is in Psalm 113:5-6: "Who is like the LORD our God, the One who sits enthroned on high, who stoops down to look on the heavens and the earth?" There are twenty-eight other uses of the Hebrew word for stooped down, but those all refer to people being brought low, not to God.

I like to keep this image of Jesus bringing down the temperature of a heated situation in mind when I think about responding to the abortion issue. Grace means I can take a breath, and take a second to invite him into any discussion. I can take a humble posture and let go of the need to prove anything to anyone.

I also keep in mind the way he protects the woman who was at risk of being stoned to death. The emotional reality for the majority of women facing unintended pregnancies today isn't physical life and death like it was for the woman in John 8, but they often say they feel as if their life as they know it is over. And that feeling of shame doesn't always go away. Any time I'm in a conversation about abortion, I don't know if someone with lived experience is also part of that conversation. By my demeanor and attitude, by the way I elevate grace, I can create a similar buffer, ensuring I don't contribute to any more shame.

**Second, Jesus addresses the sin of the religious people.** When Jesus does speak, it is not the answer the Pharisees are looking for. He doesn't address the legal wrongdoings of the woman. He turns the focus to the behavior of the religious leaders, saying, "Let any one of you who is without sin be the first to throw a stone at her" (John 8:7). With that directive to examine their own faults, Jesus takes the power out of their question about stoning the woman. He removes the ammunition in their attempt to trap him, and they drop their stones and leave one by one.

The Greek word for "without sin" in verse 7 is *anamartētos*, which means guiltless, one who has not sinned, *one who cannot sin*. Interestingly, it is the only time this word is used in Scripture. *Anamartētos* is derived from the more common Greek word for sin, *hamartanō*, which is used forty-three times in the New Testament and means to miss the mark, to err or be mistaken, to do or go wrong. Though translators use the English word *sin* for both of them, the Greek words carry different meanings.

The Pharisees viewed themselves as the most righteous people in society, so I'm guessing they wouldn't usually have said they were in error, wrong, or had missed the mark. They would have reserved those words for a woman committing adultery, putting her in a category far below themselves. Is it possible that John intentionally used *anamartētos*—"one who cannot sin"—because Jesus phrased this as a foreshadowing of himself as the sinless Messiah who is the only one who can cast judgment? Whatever his reason, the first words Jesus spoke went straight to the heart of a group of people who were callous enough to risk the life of a woman in order to get what they wanted. He asked the religious leaders to evaluate themselves using the same measure they held up to the woman.

What message have you heard Christians lead with in the abortion debate? I would have to put the word *sin* into the top responses I've heard. We most often hear Christians emphasize the errors of others— the woman seeking an abortion, lawmakers, abortion providers, abortion protestors, and the other "side." And yet, when was the last time you heard a Christian lead a conversation about abortion by evaluating their own sin?

If Jesus were here today to address our response to abortion, what would he say first? Would he start with the church, as he did with the religious leaders in this story in John? Would he first open our eyes to areas where we have missed the mark in our perspective, our talking points, our emphases, and our engagement?

The same Lifeway study that found few people approach the church before an abortion also found some reasons why:

- Sixty-four percent believe that church members are more likely to gossip about a woman considering abortion than to help her understand options.

- Fifty-two percent say that no one at their church knows about their abortion.

- Forty-nine percent say that pastors' teachings on forgiveness don't seem to apply to their terminated pregnancies.[3]

The picture painted by these perceptions is very far from the description of Jesus when he walked the earth.

***Third, Jesus refuses to condemn.*** When Jesus finally addresses the woman, he does not condemn her. We are halfway through the story before Jesus addresses the woman, yet he does it in the opposite way the Pharisees intended. They had asked him to condemn her to a possible death sentence, but Jesus tells her he does not condemn her. Does he only say that because everyone has left? Or is there something more to his proclamation?

When Jesus tells the Pharisees, "Let any one of you who is without sin cast the first stone," who is the only one without sin? He is. He's the only perfect one there. He could have thrown a stone; but he knew exactly why he had come to earth. Our gracious God came into this moment not to exercise his right to judge, but to forgive.

We find ample theological context for what we see play out in John 8 throughout the rest of the Bible. Paul's teaching in Romans 3 helps us understand *why* Jesus leveled the playing field between the Pharisees and the woman's behavior:

> For there is no difference between us and them in this. Since we've . . . proved that we are utterly incapable of living the glorious lives God wills for us, God did it for us. Out of sheer generosity he put us in right standing with himself. A pure gift. He got us out of the mess we're in and restored us to where he always wanted us to be. And he did it by means of Jesus Christ. (Romans 3:21-24 MSG)

Jesus offers concrete examples of the reality that humans tend to focus on outward behavior but God understands that even our thoughts can cause harm when we try to get our needs met at the expense of others. This puts us all on an equal playing field, even when our behavior looks vastly different.

> You have heard that it was said to those of old, "You shall not murder; and whoever murders will be liable to judgment." But I say to you that everyone who is angry with his brother will be liable to judgment; whoever insults his brother will be liable to the council. . . . You have heard that it was said, "You shall not commit adultery." But I say to you that everyone who looks at a woman with lustful intent has already committed adultery with her in his heart. (Matthew 5:21-22, 27-28 ESV)

When Jesus says to the woman, "Neither do I condemn you," his words mirror some of my favorite verses in Romans:

> Therefore, there is now no condemnation for those who are in Christ Jesus, because through Christ Jesus, the law of the Spirit who gives life has set you free from the law of sin and death. For what the law was powerless to do because it was weakened by the flesh, God did by sending his own Son in the likeness of sinful flesh to be a sin offering. And so he condemned sin in the flesh, in order that the righteous requirement of the law might be fully met in us, who do not live according to the flesh but according to the Spirit. (Romans 8:1-4)

In John 8, notice that Jesus does not condemn the Pharisees either. He is far more gracious with them than I would be. He could have named their sin, but he didn't. I wonder what that felt like for them? Did any of the Pharisees respond to Jesus' invitation to examine themselves?

I wonder what this felt like for the woman? She went from feeling condemned in every imaginable way and fearing her life was over, to having an encounter with Jesus, who extended grace. She had lived under the paradigm of the religious leaders being ultra-righteous for so long, I wonder if she was able to comprehend that Jesus was leveling the playing field. I tend to think she did, as that is the most logical explanation for her being able to grasp what Jesus says next.

*Fourth, Jesus offers a transformed life.* Last, Jesus addresses the woman by inviting her to live a transformed life. The Pharisees wanted him to address the woman first, and they wanted him to do it in a condemning way. They had no regard for her future or her wellbeing; they were motivated by their own need to appear righteous and have the upper hand. Jesus waits until they all have left to finally address the woman, and his words to her flow naturally out of all of the grace he has shown until then. By the time he tells her to "go and sin no more," she has been protected and shown love, so she can envision living a transformed life. She is receiving an invitation from someone who has seen her, valued her, and elevated her identity. This is the biblical model for how any of us change.

There is a chronology of grace in Jesus' response to the woman (and in Paul's teachings in his epistles) where we see a pattern of *grace first*. In her 2012 TED Talk, "The Power of Vulnerability," Brené Brown describes how her research on shame and vulnerability distinguishes between *guilt* and *shame* in a way relevant to this order of grace first. She says experiencing guilt is about our behavior: "I made a mistake." Shame is about our identity: "I am a mistake." She goes on to say that shame is highly correlated with all types of destructive behaviors, because we are acting out of this negative identity.

This research aligns well with the framework of *grace first*. We learn what God does for us before we act in response. It means that in God's economy, the motivation for our transformation isn't "You must leave your life of sin," but rather "Because of grace, it's possible for you to leave your life of sin. You *get* to do that."

## Grace Replaces Bias with Curiosity
### —*Krysta Masciale*

I remember going to abortion clinics to picket with my mom when I was four years old. I held a sign that said, "I love babies." I was exposed to pro-life pamphlets that were graphic and certainly not age appropriate. Growing up in the Bible Belt, I inherited the idea that to love Jesus was to be anti-abortion and pro-life. I didn't understand what that actually meant, but I knew it included assumptions about the kind of person who would find themselves in a situation where they were facing an unintended pregnancy.

Abortion wasn't a topic I chose to question critically, because I didn't think it concerned me. And here's where I was wrong: As a follower of Christ, I don't need to experience injustices, oppression, or dehumanization in order to step into that space and offer God's grace. In fact, I'm called to do so regardless of my lived experience, and I do so by asking questions and living in proximity to those who have different experiences than I have.

Prior to having children, I often judged women in the workplace for leaving early to pick up their kids from school without even realizing that they came in two hours before me. I absorbed the myth that to be a mom meant you were less useful and less committed to your work. Becoming a mom unlocked a flood of biases I held toward myself, because I had internalized the communal rhetoric that women weren't valued if their behavior wasn't perfect. I often felt isolated in those early days of motherhood because I thought I alone had to make decisions; I wasn't taught that men were also a part of the equation.

Becoming a mom isn't a prerequisite to understanding the complexities of unintended pregnancy, but it did help me understand. We have failed women and we have failed our churches when we form opinions about people in the name of Jesus without first understanding the full story of their experience. I started to see the full story when I saw ProGrace's research on women's experiences with unintended pregnancy. Once I started opening up to their experiences, I started digging for real social solutions.

What I didn't anticipate as I interacted with ProGrace's work was the shift I experienced in my own relationship with Jesus and the new lens through which I began to see the world. I found my faith on a fast track to maturity because I was learning the discipline of asking better questions. I became free of the tension that came with tying my faith to anti-anything. What's most freeing about my experience with ProGrace is that I've learned to bring grace and curiosity into conversations that are trying to dehumanize anyone in our society. This gives me confidence that I'm actually reflecting the heart of God.

---

*Krysta Masciale is an executive leader in operations strategy and lives in Los Angeles with her two children and husband.*

# 3

# Grace and Truth
# Are Not Contradictory

I WAS STANDING IN THE SANCTUARY of a historic church in Chicago, facilitating a workshop on the ProGrace approach, when someone in the back raised their hand. "But, what about grace and truth?" This event was one of many workshops we piloted with churches in Chicago while I was leading the pregnancy organization and beginning to take the ProGrace message to churches, and it was one of many times I received this question.

I'm not going to lie; the question irked me. It got under my skin. I knew the subtext was, "But when do we tell her that having an abortion is wrong?" I didn't have an answer, and I didn't want to just stumble my way through like I had before. Finally, on this particular night, I paused long enough to whisper in my spirit to God, *I'm so sick of this question. What should I say?*

Immediately, another question popped into my head: "What truth would you tell her first?" So I said to the group, "Based on what you know about a woman's experience when facing an unintended pregnancy, what truth would you tell her first?" After a very short pause, the majority of the group gave a unified response: "That God loves her."

The group wasn't trying to condemn women; they were caught in a false binary. And just like me, they needed the Spirit to reframe their thinking.

## WHAT TRUTH DO WE NEED TO HEAR FIRST

I grew up in a church that believed we could lose our salvation if we moved far enough away from God. The pastor would pace the stage, his voice rising to a near yell, and pound his fist on the podium as he told us all that God required. Most of the sermons were from the Old Testament or the epistles of Paul. I don't remember sermons from the first half of the epistles, where Paul outlines our identity in Christ and all God has done for us. Most often, the pastor would skip right to the second half on how we should live.

As a young girl, I absorbed the belief that God required a lot from me, which caused me to feel anxious, worried I was never doing it quite right. I wanted to love Jesus, but wondered if I was loving him enough. I wasn't taught the beautiful fullness of grace, which God initiates and sustains. My understanding of Christianity was that it was about my effort. A counselor told me the "bend of my bow" was set to performance because of my formative years, and I felt like there was a blockage between my head and my heart. I could hear teachings about God's love and cognitively understand, but I didn't experience it. I asked God over and over to change that.

When we started attending the Vineyard church, we were introduced to a spiritual practice called listening prayer. This means the prayer team is trained to wait on the Holy Spirit and try to sense God's unique heart for each person. Every time I went for prayer those first several years, it was like a broken record: "The Father wants you to know how much he loves you." "You are the beloved daughter, and God is so pleased with you." "I pray you can more deeply grasp the love of the Father."

This was the truth I needed to hear first. I needed to hear it over and over and over again. I knew a lot of truths about God before this, but none could really take root until I accepted this one, and it changed my entire experience of Christianity.

## GOD'S LOVE IS BIGGER

When we are struggling, what do we need to hear first? We need to hear that struggle, making mistakes, and failure are common to the human condition. We need to hear that God's love for us is bigger than any of those. When people ask me "What about grace and truth?" they are operating from the paradigm that truth is always about pointing out what God is *against*. For some Christians, that can different things: Either God is *against* abortion, or God is *against* limiting women's autonomy, or God is *against* us trying to legislate morality.

But the truth that comes through Jesus is also about what God is *for*.

- He is first and foremost *for* love.

- He is *for* the value, dignity, and worth of each person he has created.

- He is *for* listening, understanding, and extending grace to the human experience, in all its complexities.

- He is *for* his church being an approachable community of healing and belonging that resembles Christ.

Grace reveals the truth that God is motivated by love in all of his actions toward humanity; it is the demonstration that God's desire to have a loving relationship with people is more important to him than the most destructive of our behaviors and thoughts. It is also the pathway to becoming who we were created to be.

> But the gracious gift is not like the offense. For if by the offense of the one [Adam] the many died, much more did the grace of God and the gift by the grace of the one Man, Jesus Christ, *overflow* to the many. . . . For if by the offense of the one, death reigned through the one [Adam], much more will those who receive the *abundance* of grace and of the gift of righteousness reign in life through the One, Jesus Christ. . . . The Law came in so that the offense would increase; but where sin increased, grace *abounded* all the more, so that, as sin reigned in death, so also grace would reign through righteousness to eternal life through Jesus Christ our Lord. (Romans 5:15, 17, 20-21 NASB 2020, emphasis added)

The words *overflow*, *abundance*, and *abounded* all share the same Greek root word, *perisseuō*, which means to be left over and above a certain number or measure. It's the same word used to describe the twelve baskets of food that were left over after Jesus multiplied loaves and fish to feed five thousand people (Mark 6:30-44). The "measure" in that story was five thousand men plus women and children, and Jesus exceeded it. The "measure" in Romans 5 is the sin of Adam and the impact of sin on all of humanity as we try to get our needs met in ways that harm ourselves and others. God's grace is more than enough and above and beyond what is needed to address this.

## OUR MODEL FOR GRACE AND TRUTH

There are two times "grace and truth" appear in the Bible, and they are used to describe Jesus or his ministry.

We have seen his glory, the glory of the one and only Son, who came from the Father, full of grace and truth. (John 1:14)

Grace and truth came through Jesus Christ. (John 1:17)

This means the two terms aren't contradictory, they don't need to balance each other out, and they are both perfectly demonstrated in Jesus. So we must look to Jesus as our primary example for what these concepts look like in practice.

When we examine Jesus' ministry, we find numerous examples of how he highlights what God is for. He also at times speaks truth about what God is against; however, Jesus does not lead with these truths when he encounters those who are vulnerable, struggling, or feeling marginalized. We see him express anger and reveal harmful behavior and thoughts primarily when people abuse power, particularly religious power. Consider this passage:

Woe to you, scribes and Pharisees, hypocrites! For you tithe mint and dill and cumin, and have neglected the weightier matters of the law: justice and mercy and faithfulness. These you ought to have done, without neglecting the others. You blind guides, straining out a gnat and swallowing a camel!

Woe to you, scribes and Pharisees, hypocrites! For you clean the outside of the cup and the plate, but inside they are full of greed and self-indulgence. You blind Pharisee! First clean the inside of the cup and the plate, that the outside also may be clean. (Matthew 23:23-26 ESV)

Many Christians in the United States have been taught that our most important responsibility in regard to abortion is to communicate what God is against. This makes it hard for us to reconcile the idea of grace and truth existing together, in perfect harmony. If we believe we primarily need to point out negative behavior instead of communicating the truth of the love of God that Jesus modeled, we are believing a half-truth that gravely misses the point of how God interacts with humanity and brings change. It is a diminished view of Jesus. Throughout Jesus' ministry, he revealed the truth that God sees each person, prioritizes healing them above playing into the power structures of their society, and loves them without fail.

## GRACE REVEALS THE FULL TRUTH

A volunteer at a church was leading a support group for women during and after unintended pregnancy, to welcome them into the church and provide a safe community. During this time, one of the pastors' teenage daughters became pregnant, and the church staff decided to discontinue the group for pregnant women and single moms. They felt that having the group was sending the wrong message to the youth of the church about sexual activity outside of marriage, and that it could make it difficult to uphold what they believed to be true about God's intent.

By focusing only on the women facing unintended pregnancy, this church wasn't engaging with the whole truth of their convictions. For leaders in the church to truly disciple their congregation into what they believed was God's design for sexuality within marriage, they would have needed to recognize just how many people needed that discipleship—including the men involved in unintended pregnancies, and ultimately everyone in the church.

And this half-truth caused real damage. Women who were parenting alone no longer had the support of the group, and the church was seen as hypocritical for not focusing on everyone's sexuality. Any young woman who did get pregnant would interpret this as an example that the church wasn't safe to approach for help. I don't think this is the message they were intending to send, but their actions reinforced what the Lifeway study found: Judgment and lack of support are the primary reasons women don't approach anyone at a church when considering abortion.[1]

When we look at the ministry of Jesus, we see a different picture. People who were ostracized from their religious community consistently and boldly approached Jesus and followed him. Being embraced by Jesus, just as they were, shifted their sense of identity, and they could not help but be changed. This is grace, and it is how we all are transformed. So why are we often tempted to hide parts of ourselves we feel are unacceptable? Could it be that we don't yet believe the whole truth of grace?

While most Christians agree that the church should be a welcoming place for all people, the reality is that we—like much of humanity—have often failed in this calling. Historically, churches have turned people away based on race, gender, or perceived moral standing, despite the message of equality and belonging at the heart of the gospel.

A space is only truly welcoming when it is safe for all people. When I say "safe," I mean physically and emotionally safe. We may disagree when defining what is emotionally safe or unsafe, but we can agree that we all share the same basic needs for belonging, connection, and understanding. We feel safe in communities where these needs are met, and the church is only able to meet these needs when we move forward in the whole truth that grace reveals, prioritizing people over politics.

## The Limitless Love of the Father
### —David Gregg

My wife and I have eight kids total—two biological and six adopted through foster care over the years. Our two biological daughters were born when I was fifteen and seventeen years old.

Being fifteen in high school with a kid on the way doesn't go well—not with your peers, and not with your teachers. I had one teacher pull me aside and tell me, "Hey, if you could keep it in your pants, this wouldn't be a problem," and that didn't feel good. I struggled trying to balance school and also get a job to start preparing financially for our child. I didn't have friend time, so friends kind of disappeared. That drop in support network was hard, and so was hearing my parents' disappointment when I explained to them what was happening.

Our families stepped up to support, and our experience would have been a lot harder if they hadn't. We lived with my in-laws for a couple of years while we got on our feet, and they were instrumental in helping us get financially sound.

We weren't part of a Christian community at the time; my daughters are actually what brought me to Christ. I grew up with an abusive father, and I wanted to learn how to be a good dad to my kids. This was pre-internet, and I didn't have any books to read, but I had a Bible. I started reading it, and that's how I learned about our Heavenly Father. We started attending a local church after our first daughter was born, and when we had our second daughter, they kicked us out of the church.

I hope for my kids to live a life with their spouse as God would intend—loving and in unity. I also want them to know that if they encounter trouble, we are here for them, that we're going to support them regardless of what they're going through. Our second daughter and her husband got married right out of high school, went on a mission trip, and came back pregnant. Rather than responding with negativity about them not being old or mature enough, we celebrated with them, embracing that there's life coming into the world, because that's what our God is about. He is life and love.

When I make a mistake, what I want from someone else is for them to help pick me back up. I don't want to be kicked down further. So when we see a person who has had an experience that is taking them down a notch, we don't want them to stay there. We want to help, and we're not going to do it through the law; we're going to do it ourselves. And we've seen that this actually works.

---

*David Gregg serves as a deacon at LIFE Community Church in North Carolina, where he trains church members to create a safe environment for people experiencing unintended pregnancy.*

# 4

# Transcending Partisan Politics

IN THE EARLY DAYS OF PROGRACE, we used a visual of a cliff to illustrate our country's political divide around abortion. On one side were people holding signs depicting a woman; on the other were people holding signs depicting a child. I was sharing this image with a pro-choice woman when she told me, "I'm offended that you are portraying pro-choice people as anti-child. I've worked in maternal child health my entire career, advocating for the welfare of children."

I apologized and told her we hadn't meant to communicate pro-choice people were anti-child. Then I asked her if she also disagreed with the opposite assumption—that pro-life people were anti-woman. "Oh no," she told me, "that is absolutely true."

Even though I don't usually hear it said quite this explicitly, this is the subtext of many political conversations today. We don't think we fit the stereotypes of our political side, but we consciously or subconsciously assign stereotypes to people on the other side. It's easy to see the faults in someone we disagree with, but much harder to recognize faults in our own communities. Even if we believe we are the "exception" to our political party, most people won't view us that way. Unless the person knows us well and we have a lot of positive history together, they will assign us all the stereotypes of our political camp.

When we lead conversations with our political view on abortion, we are making it more likely for our listeners to assign us a stereotype. If we say we are pro-life, many people will hear that we are anti-woman. If we say we are pro-choice, many people will hear that we are anti-child. This is an unfortunate reality, as most people do not fit neatly into the stereotypes of their political party, but it's a reality we must be aware of. Whenever the political stances of Christians communicate that God cares less about anyone made in his image, even when that is far from our intent, we have a problem.

## NOT A ZERO-SUM GAME

When my colleagues and I first started changing some of the practices at our pregnancy organization to be more woman-centric, a fellow executive director requested a meeting to tell me I was on a "slippery slope to becoming pro-choice." Her rationale was that if we were elevating the needs of the woman, we would naturally begin to decrease our concern for the needs of the child. Inversely, several people over the years have told me that when their friends or pastors read the ProGrace vision and mission, they wondered if we were just "pro-life light." When they read that we wanted to work for the equal dignity and welfare of both the woman and the child, they interpreted that to mean our primary focus was still the child, but we were going to be nicer about it than extreme pro-life rhetoric.

Both examples illuminate a common human fear that as we call attention to and work for the just treatment of people, we are playing a zero-sum game where one person's gain is another person's loss. This cautionary view is understandable in the limiting context of abortion legislation, which does currently mandate we elevate the interests of one party over the other. But if we as Christians can enter the abortion conversation with a solid belief that justice in the kingdom of God is *not* a zero-sum game, we can be honest about the fact that there are values and talking points on both political sides that align with his heart. We see this in the gospels, when the Pharisees bring Jesus a problem or question. They try to trap him by focusing myopically on one controversial topic, sometimes a political lightning rod, that will divide people. And Jesus responds by speaking to the broader truth of God's value for humanity.

The partisan talking points around abortion today are not too dissimilar from the myopic topics the Pharisees brought to Jesus. Though there are beautiful truths about caring for people within both political platforms, stereotypes prevail because each platform excludes meaningful questions about the other person involved.

Neither political platform allows sufficient space to wrestle with the complexity of what it would mean to work for the dignity and welfare of both people. They mobilize us to vote by exaggerating our differences and demonizing the other "side," without prioritizing laws that would support people facing unintended pregnancy or considering abortion. (Thankfully, there has been some progress on bipartisan legislation, as the Pregnant Workers' Fairness Act passed in 2022, after ten years of focused effort to get the necessary votes.)

Even when we limit the terms *pro-life* and *pro-choice* to their political context rather than a moral standing rooted in religious convictions, people still interpret these terms differently. As a result, it remains unclear what it is that those who use these terms actually want to be legalized. For example, the Mississippi Gestational Act (HB 1510)—which was at the center of the *Dobbs v. Jackson* case and led to *Roe* being overturned—illustrates this complexity.[1] That act prohibited abortion after fifteen weeks, except for medical emergencies or severe fetal abnormalities. It was challenged because *Roe v. Wade* guaranteed that states could regulate, but not outlaw, abortions up until fetal viability (defined as the end of the second trimester, or twenty-seven weeks).

For context, 93 percent of abortions in the United States are before thirteen weeks. Another 6 percent happen between weeks fourteen and twenty, and about 1 percent are at twenty-one weeks or beyond.[2] Today, fifty years after *Roe*, most experts consider fetal viability to be around twenty-four weeks. It can be confusing for people who are not involved in politics to determine whether a law that banned abortions after fifteen weeks—allowing about 93 percent of abortions to continue—would be considered pro-life or pro-choice. This is one example that illustrates how insufficient the terms are for fostering productive conversation around abortion.

## SPACE FOR NUANCE

Most Christians, whether pro-life or pro-choice, have nuanced policy views that incorporate a concern for both the woman and the child, but we often don't reach that place of common ground in our conversations because we lead with partisan labels which don't hold space for nuance. Unfortunately, in today's divisive environment, when we say we align with a party, it signals to the other side that we don't share their values and are unsafe for having this conversation.

Becoming prograce does not mean decreasing our commitment to just laws—I hope it strengthens that commitment. Researching candidates and voting thoughtfully in local and national elections are essential parts of living in a democracy, and political engagement is a meaningful way to care for others and steward the world.

Becoming prograce means embracing a fuller view of God's value for every person and shifting our ultimate hope from partisan politics—which often fails to bring lasting change—toward God's redemptive plan, which involves a unified church.

## HAVE WE GIVEN TO THE GOVERNMENT WHAT IS GOD'S?

Then, the Pharisees went out and laid plans to trap him in his words. They sent their disciples to him along with the Herodians.

"Teacher," they said, "we know that you are a man of integrity and that you teach the way of God in accordance with the truth. You aren't swayed by others because you pay no attention to who they are. Tell us then, what is your opinion? Is it right to pay the imperial tax to Caesar or not?"

But Jesus, knowing their evil intent, said, "You hypocrites, why are you trying to trap me? Show me the coin used for paying the tax." They brought him a denarius, and he asked them, "Whose image is this? And whose inscription?"

"Caesar's," they replied.

Then he said to them, "So give back to Caesar what is Caesar's, and to God what is God's." (Matthew 22:15-21)

The Pharisees' question in this story was laser-focused on a hot topic: imperial taxes. If Jesus said it was right to pay taxes to Caesar, he would inflame the very people he came to teach and lead, and they would turn away from following him. If he said it wasn't right, the Romans could have arrested him for sedition against Herod, the puppet ruler of Israel, and ended his teaching ministry.

The people listening to Jesus spent much time lamenting the brutal oppression of their Roman occupiers. But in one sentence, Jesus puts Rome into its rightful place—below God—and opens up a whole new way of thinking about their situation: Their real citizenship was in the kingdom of God.

Christians have a rich historical heritage of caring for people when governments did not. Early Christians in the Roman empire lived out their kingdom citizenship by rescuing Roman infants who were left to die. Christians were known to care for people suffering from plagues long before governments developed healthcare or medical support. While many people avoided the sick out of fear of dying, Christians moved toward them, unafraid of death and motivated to demonstrate God's love. Many scholars believe these actions were a critical factor in the growth of the church.[3] In his book *The Rise of*

*Christianity*, sociologist Rodney Stark examines both Christian and Roman records that show Christians were significantly more active than their neighbors in caring for the sick during two major epidemics in the second and third centuries, even at significant personal risk, with some of them losing their lives. They also engaged more in caregiving outside of epidemics. By the fourth century, the church's growth had become so concerning to the Roman Emperor Julian that he established charities to rival these caregiving efforts and counter Christian expansion.

In a roundabout way, these Christians influenced their government to better support those in need by elevating their citizenship in the kingdom of God. This rich Christian heritage is reflected today in countless individuals who dedicate their lives to caring for others, regardless of the help they do or don't receive from their government. What might it look like for us to embody this commitment in our current circumstances?

This doesn't mean we abdicate our democratic responsibilities. Unlike Christians under Roman occupation, we actually can vote for policies that provide care to people who need it. We can tangibly impact the reality of abortion in our country by advocating for policies that better support women and children through healthcare, paid maternity leave, and supplemented childcare costs. We don't do this out of blind allegiance to a particular political party that claims those issues as its own. Instead, we seek to do it as the Christians who have gone before us: As kingdom citizens, following Christ to bring his hope to a world filled with systemic brokenness.

## THE IMPACT OF RELYING ON POLITICS

While it's important to remember this privilege, our democracy can make it easy to think of laws as the primary answer to important ethical issues—that's more straightforward than taking the time and courage to look inside ourselves and ask if we are becoming more like Jesus, to corporately become the community we need to be to help when people are in struggle. It is crucial for us to vote and engage our culture. But laws that permit or ban abortion are not designed to build a community that can facilitate grace-led conversations, view the issue holistically, and value and support women and children equally; the church is intended to be that community. If we place the bulk of our confidence, focus, and energy into the legality or illegality of abortion, we give the government a role that is rightfully God's. The US church now has a fifty-year history of communicating a primarily political approach to abortion, and the following are some of the consequences.

*We are divided as Christians.* After *Roe v. Wade* was overturned in June 2022, many pastors and leaders were at a loss regarding how to address the event in their church. They had suspected their congregants were split before this decision, but many weren't prepared for how vocal people on both sides would become. People were shocked to see the responses their Christian friends posted on social media, questioning if they could even continue to have them over for dinner. Pastors got emails criticizing them if they celebrated the decision too much or didn't celebrate it enough. Parents looked for common-ground ways to talk to their teenage and adult children.

*People with lived experience don't tend to approach churches.* The percentage of those in the United States in general who trust church and organized religion is near an all-time low at 32 percent.[4] Public trust of pastors fell for the third year in a row to a historic low of 34 percent, down from 67 percent in 1985.[5] When women who don't attend church were asked how they anticipated churches would have responded if they had approached them before their abortion decision, 7 percent said caring, 7 percent said helpful, and 6 percent said loving.[6] Of regular churchgoing women who have had abortions, only 38 percent say anyone at their church knows about their experience and less than two in five believe pastors are sensitive to the realities of an unintended pregnancy.[7]

I know so many pastors who deeply desire to change these statistics, to communicate value for women, and to speak peace to their congregation on divisive issues. This is incredibly difficult, and especially so with abortion, which for so long has been laden with shame in Christian settings. When our only option is to walk the razor-thin tightrope between the political divide, we risk alienating each other and compounding this shame. We can come across as valuing policy over people, which is the natural result of approaching a human issue from a limiting legal context.

***Younger generations are leaving the church.*** Research from 2024 found that 69 percent of US Americans born between 1925 and 1945 identified as Christian and 19 percent as "none." "None" includes atheist, agnostic, and those who may be spiritual but not interested in organized religion. Among the youngest Americans (those born starting in 1996 and old enough to be surveyed in 2024), 36 percent are Christians, and 46 percent identified as none.[8] According to associate professor of political science, Ryan Burge, this generation is "the first generation in American history in which the nones clearly outnumber the Christians."[9]

Though the most recent Pew Research Center religious study found that "after many years of steady decline, the share of Americans who identify as Christians shows signs of leveling off," they also made this prediction:

In future years we may see further declines in the religiousness of the American public, for several reasons:

- Young adults are far less religious than older adults.

- No recent birth cohort has become more religious as it has aged.

- The "stickiness" of a religious upbringing seems to be declining: Compared with older people, fewer young adults who had a highly religious upbringing are still highly religious as adults.

- The "stickiness" of a nonreligious upbringing seems to be rising.[10]

There are also changes happening between genders when it comes to religious affiliation. Historically, men have been more likely to claim no religious affiliation than women. But for anyone born in 1980 or later, that gender gap has disappeared. And when we look at those born around 2000, over half of women identify as "none" compared to 40 percent of men.[11] Burge notes that researchers use many data points to measure religious affiliation, so we must be careful before jumping to conclusions. What we can know is that, for decades, women ranked higher than men on church attendance and affiliation, and that gender gap has narrowed significantly for young adults. It's difficult to know exactly why this shift is happening, but Burge is confident politics play a role.[12] If we listen to young women describe their experience with Christians and the church, we often hear they are disillusioned because of the way the church has handled issues that directly impact women, including abortion.

A woman in the ProGrace community told us about her daughter who experienced hurt from the church and now doesn't attend one regularly. Her daughter decided to visit a church in her college town the Sunday after *Roe v. Wade* was overturned. The pastor spent several minutes celebrating the decision and how it could affect their state law, without mentioning any corresponding policies or support programs for pregnant women and single-parent families. This young woman felt disturbed thinking about how the political framing would affect women with lived experience of unintended pregnancy or abortion, and she eventually walked out of the church.

When we frame complex human situations primarily as "issues" to be handled in the political sphere, it is dangerously easy to disregard the humans who are impacted by them. This is the theological shortcoming of simply aligning our abortion response around the either/or framing of our political parties. Acknowledging this shortcoming is the first step in "giving to Caesar what is Caesar's and to God what is God's."

| What Does Belong to God? | | |
|---|---|---|
| Hope | Love | Grace |
| Life | Community | Care |

The church's anxiety and perceived helplessness around abortion render too much authority to the government and not enough to God. Policies surrounding abortion *are* important to discuss, vote on, and even seek to change. But when Christians collectively make a *political* stance the primary focus, we can quickly lose sight of the incredibly important ways Jesus interacted with people in need.

US Americans in the twenty-first century are starting to see the limits of our political responsibility in a way that's different from the generations before us. We have experience with abortion becoming legal on a national level for fifty years, then changing to a state-by-state decision. We have no assurance what will happen politically in the next several years.

What remains constant through all of this change is the nature of God, made manifest in Jesus, and the "revolution of character" he calls us into. Our shared values of human dignity and grace can be anchors for the church in a rapidly changing political landscape where we cannot trust all humans will be cared for. Regardless of who holds political power and what they choose to do with it, we as the church are able to follow Jesus. This is a radical gift, relief, and responsibility.

## Choosing Connection over Certainty
### —Barb White

Recently, my mother passed away at age eighty-two. Throughout her life, she took on many roles, but her greatest pride came from advocating for women's health and reproductive rights in the late 1970s. As I grew and developed my own faith, I found myself at odds with some of her beliefs. Navigating this tension was difficult, especially as I became more involved in church life. When my husband joined the staff of a church, the ideologies around sex, abortion, and child-rearing were particularly strong.

At the same time, I worked with high school students, both as a teacher and a youth group volunteer. I saw the challenges they faced: Some were sexually active, some considered abortions, others carried pregnancies to term, and many kept secrets from their parents. My mother's generation had one set of beliefs; the parents of my students had another; and the students were still forming their own views. In the midst of it all, I felt torn—both conflicted and compassionate.

When I learned about ProGrace, I felt a sense of relief and peace. It reminded me that we can hold two truths at once: we can be safe, loving people without fully understanding someone else's experiences. Our role isn't to have all the answers but to be present and loving, focusing on relationships over being "right." Partnering with Jesus means choosing to know and care for our neighbors rather than rushing to judge or assume we know best.

One of the biggest problems is that, too often, we prioritize institutions and certainty over relationships and love. Conversations get derailed by fear—fear of being wrong or losing power and control—leaving little room for genuine connection. The church has often mirrored this, with people parroting institutional stances instead of embracing the messy, grace-filled approach of walking with others, as Jesus did. The world is full of gray areas, and we aren't called to navigate them with certitude, but with humility and grace. In loving our neighbors, listening, and learning, we find the true essence of following Jesus.

*Barb White is a leadership coach and consultant based in the Midwest who worked in public education for over twenty-five years.*

PART 2

# The Complexities of Abortion

# 5

# Listening to Women

In 2008, I gathered with several colleagues in a downtown Chicago conference room to hear the results of research we had commissioned with our pregnancy organization clients. The specific question I wanted that research to answer was: Why do women have abortions?

Going into this research, I had already studied the quantitative research that existed in the United States. These numbers include:

- At current rates, one in four women will have an abortion in their lifetime.[1]

- About 95 percent of abortions are for an unintended pregnancy.[2]

- Just over 40 percent of all pregnancies are unintended.[3]

- Around 85 percent of women who have abortions are unmarried.[4]

- Approximately six in ten women seeking abortion have given birth to one or more children.[5]

When surveyed why they chose abortion, the most common reasons women give are:

- financial (40 percent)
- timing (36 percent)
- partner (31 percent)
- needs of other children (29 percent)

Most women (64 percent) give more than one reason, which makes sense considering the overlap between these four reasons.[6] For example, timing is most likely tied to financial and/or relational stability. We could categorize all four reasons as lack of emotional and practical support.

Over the years, I found a good amount of quantitative data about unintended pregnancy, but barely any qualitative data, which describes the situation from the perspectives of individuals and looks for repetitive themes instead of numbers. Where quantitative data tells us the *what* of a given topic, qualitative data seeks to answer *why*.

## LISTENING THROUGH RESEARCH

The research we commissioned is a unique type of qualitative research called Emotional Inquiry® which involves one-on-one interviews and relies on a relatively small sample size. The sample size for Emotional Inquiry® is small because emotional drivers tend to be more universal; emotionally, people are more similar than different. In the research, "respondents are guided through relaxation and visualization exercises and respond to a series of probes about experiences in their past and how they feel as they recall the times, places and people involved."[7] Their responses are recorded and analyzed to help researchers understand the emotional drivers behind their behaviors and decisions, rather than sampling their surface opinions. As with all research, it does not definitively state what the experience is like for all women, and it is important that we continue to expand qualitative research in this area to better understand the experience, especially as younger generations come of age in the wake of shifting abortion legislation.

Through the unique study design, women involved in our Emotional Inquiry® research were able to access the deep emotional impact that news of an unintended pregnancy had on their sense of self, as well as the messages they received from their family and friends during the experience. I can still see myself in that room as I heard composite and verbatim quotes from the interviews highlighting women's experiences of unintended pregnancy. At one point, we heard a direct quote from a woman who said, "I felt so stupid. That's what I thought others would think—that I was stupid or dumb." I had a visceral response when I heard the word "stupid." I thought, *It's not right that she would carry that feeling of shame over this.* I knew what it felt like to be judged around my reproduction, and by this point I also knew that those judgments were based on lies. It pained me on a soul level to hear other women being harmed by similar messages, and I wanted all of the women we worked with to experience the same value, care, and freedom I worked so hard to believe in for myself.

Since 2008, we've commissioned three more bodies of research and discovered that, even though our political and cultural landscape is shifting, the experience of unintended pregnancy continues to have many realities that are shared across diverse socioeconomic groups, ages, and geographic locations (within the United States). The common denominator between the women who participated in the research was that they were seeking emotional support and/or practical resources from a nonprofit pregnancy organization. Many of them had also visited other practitioners, such as physicians and Planned Parenthood, for medical care, consultation, and abortion. Each group included women who had chosen to parent, to place for adoption, and to have an abortion, and in all four bodies of research, the researchers were not informed of what decision each woman had made before their interview. Regardless of what decision they made, the insights from the research on their emotional experiences of unintended pregnancy were consistent across the samples.

Throughout fifty women's stories, we heard that when a woman finds out she's pregnant and wasn't intending to be, she often enters into a fracture of her identity, separated immediately from the person she knew herself to be. The way she thought about herself or imagined her future is gone, but she doesn't have a new story to replace it with yet, so she doesn't know how to feel about herself. In addition, she's often getting many messages from the world, whether perceived or actual, that communicate shame and judgment: That she's stupid, reckless, and worth less than she was before. This sense of moral lacking that a woman can experience applies whether or not she is from any type of faith background.

She is frequently afraid to tell people about the pregnancy because of the judgment and disappointment she anticipates. This can cause her to become isolated, experience a real or a perceived fracture in many key relationships, and disconnect from her support structures. Often, but not always, the male partner disappears from the story. She then has to imagine her future—and the future of another person—from this place of isolation, shame, and low self-esteem, and all in a matter of weeks. Two main questions arise as she looks ahead to the future: "How do I imagine myself in these stories?" and "Do I have the resources to even enter into those stories?"

In self-reported quantitative research, women most often cite financial and practical support as primary factors that contributed to their decision, but Emotional Inquiry® reveals a pervasive narrative of shame that is a far deeper and stronger emotional driver of abortion. Below is a composite quote from our 2019 research, which is representative of all four bodies of research.

> I took the test and my first reaction was to throw up as soon as I saw it was positive. How was I going to handle this? I had always thought, "That's not gonna be me." Being pregnant meant that I was irresponsible. I felt so ashamed and embarrassed.
>
> When women get pregnant, usually people are saying "Congratulations!" But I just felt sad.
>
> I went home from the clinic that day and got in the shower for a long time and cried. I started to think about how I was giving up my twenties. I kept thinking, "What am I going to do? What will people say about me? Who will help me?"

This decision isn't about what's happening in this one year; it's eighteen years. It's your whole life, supporting another person, making sacrifices for them, doing what's best for them. It's hard to think like that.

Going through this, you get so isolated. You step away from all the people in your life. I needed help but there was no one to help me, no one I felt like I could talk to. I didn't want to tell my parents. I had a lot of people judging me—my family and others.

For a while, I did not tell anyone except for my boyfriend. He was sweet at first, comforting. He was holding me and was saying that it will be all right. But then I asked him, "What are we going to do?" and that's when he gets mad at me. He's yelling at me: "Obviously we're not ready for this! There's no choice!" He's telling me that there's no choice; I have to get an abortion. I felt so sad, and mad at myself because I'm causing a big conflict. I remember thinking that I would have the abortion just for the sake of how he feels about me . . . how mad he was that I was pregnant. It breaks down the way you feel about yourself a lot.

We were not ready to have a kid, but I did not want to have an abortion. What I realized is that I change my life forever by keeping the child or I change my life forever by getting an abortion. I don't get to keep my life either way. It's like when my dad lost his life in a car accident: He was around one day and the next he was gone. This was the same type of sadness and emotion when I thought about abortion.

But then there was a big part of me that still wanted to have the abortion. I did not have the resources I needed, and I didn't see any way I could get what I needed. It seemed impossible.

Even though I'm a nurturing person, I did not feel cut out to handle all of it. A mom needs support, sharing, counseling. She needs help, diapers, classes about parenting. You need somebody to listen. It may not even be about how much help you get, but you need someone to *talk with*.

If you talk to your partner then you have to include how they are feeling. If you talk to your mom you have to deal with all her disappointment. But the woman I talked to at the Women's Center was a stranger, and I felt like she was going to be supportive either way. I felt like they didn't look down on me; no one there did. They don't judge you; they look after you and check on you to make sure that you're okay. It's nice to have a place that does those types of things for you.

After that day, I went to talk to my Aunt. I told her and she hugged me and that helped a lot. She had been through a similar situation in her life. It made it easier to calm down and let the stress go away for a little while. I told her I had no idea how I could take care of a child. But she said it was okay, that she was there for me, she would help. She said we would do it together. She *accepted me. She did not judge my situation. She said to me, "You can do this."*

For a lot of my life and especially when I got pregnant, it felt like God was not there. I think I pushed it away so it would not make me feel judged. It would make an already hard decision even harder. I had been told that God does not give things to people that they cannot handle, so if I turned to him he would tell me I could handle it, but everyone else was telling me that I could not handle it. So I pushed the idea of God away.

But throughout this whole experience, the people who supported me were Christians. Strangers can be kind. There are good people out there. It felt empowering. It felt like I probably had more people in my corner than I realized. Sometimes you don't realize the impact gestures have. Simple acts of diapers and a blanket and "see you next time" said to me that everything was going to be okay. That is the big need. That was enough. It told me that God is in other people.

What women have said over and over, every time we've done this research, is that they needed someone to talk to who would be open, nonjudgmental, and who would give them space to process without bringing an agenda into it. Even though women facing unintended pregnancy often push others away for fear of judgment, what they deeply need is connection, relationships within which they can begin to understand their identity in light of their new reality.

Listening to this research, I started to realize that many of our conversations about whether or not a woman should have access to abortion lacked this critical understanding of and compassion for the life-altering emotional experience of an unintended pregnancy.

## REPRODUCTIVE STORIES

Dr. Janet Jaffe, a clinical psychologist working in the field of reproductive psychology, coined the term "reproductive story" to describe the thoughts, feelings, and expectations we hold around reproduction and parenthood. All humans have reproductive stories, even if we never have children, because of our social and family structures. For many people, we are not aware of our reproductive stories until something "goes wrong" in our life related to reproduction. Dr. Jaffe explores this dynamic in the context of infertility and pregnancy loss in her book *Reproductive Trauma*. Like other forms of trauma, reproductive trauma can deeply destabilize our sense of self and sense of safety in the world. We hear this reflected in the stories of so many women who describe the "death of self" they experience when learning about an unintended pregnancy, whether or not they carry the pregnancy to term.

In addition to the unique cultural narrative of shame around an unintended pregnancy, a woman is also confronted with her own reproductive story as well as those of the people around her. In many cases, her lived experience is now standing in contradiction to the expectations she, her partner, or her community had about what that experience should look like. This can create an overwhelming sense of grief and compound her feelings of isolation.

## LISTENING TO WHAT END?

My internal reasons for listening compassionately to women who experience unintended pregnancy have changed over the years. My initial motivation for commissioning the first body of research was to understand why abortion seemed like the only option for the women we interviewed. I intended to use their answers to create programs that would meet their needs in holistic and meaningful ways— and ultimately lead to more empowered, positive outcomes for both women and children. I was not prepared for the level of transformation that would happen within me as I listened more deeply to women with this lived experience. I found that even though I didn't share their stories, I could relate to the emotions they expressed and their feelings of being crushed under unrealistic expectations of women.

When I propose listening to women as a way the church can become more like Jesus, it's helpful to expand this listening to include all reproductive stories. Part of why we haven't fully understood unintended pregnancy and abortion is that we haven't fully understood the emotional nature of reproductive loss. The less we understand the full picture, the easier it is to make faulty assumptions instead of having a holistic viewpoint and approach. The end goal of our listening is not to influence the people we listen to, but rather to be influenced ourselves by their experience and the connection we share.

## Being Present and Respecting Complexity
### —*Ginny Lupka, LCPC*

As a therapist, I care for individuals and couples navigating the impact different parts of reproduction have on their mental health. That can include anything from infertility, loss, pregnancy, postpartum, birth trauma, unintended pregnancies, or abortions. Because each of these experiences can prompt an experience of grief, they can trigger profound impacts on our health and relationships.

We all have a story around reproduction that is based on the way people talked about reproduction in our family and community of origin. Those narratives, along with other factors like our spiritual beliefs, gender and sexuality, financial resources, social support, medical concerns, and career goals, inform the expectations and values we have around reproduction as an adult.

We are often unaware of these expectations until we have a lived experience that does not meet them, and this process can be very painful. We don't just grieve the event; we grieve the internal narrative of how it was supposed to go. Understanding this can help us find empathy for others, even if we haven't had the same experience, by stepping out of our own story—in this case, our reproductive story—into someone else's.

As humans, we tend to move quickly toward problem-solving or judgment because it is uncomfortable to sit with people when they are experiencing complex and difficult things. It also requires much more mental and emotional capacity to hold conflicting values and perspectives. We gravitate toward black-and-white thinking because it feels safer than the lack of clarity found in the gray zone, but that kind of thinking dismisses the reality of how complicated the majority of life is, and it can lead us to make assumptions about others that prompt disconnection and deep hurt.

My Christian faith means I believe we are all made in the image of God. I try to utilize this lens in therapy and also in everyday life as I walk around the world, because it helps me recognize the innate dignity in my fellow humans, no matter what their life looks like. Part of human dignity is human agency, and this can really be uncomfortable to acknowledge when it comes to unintended pregnancy and abortion. To be a human made in the image of God is to be a human who is able to wrestle with decision-making in a world that is incredibly complicated.

However, we often talk in a pretty fragmented way about moral and political debate points, rather than honoring how complicated it is to navigate unintended pregnancy, both individually and as a society. Being asked to step into greater complexity is scary, because the way we've talked about this issue has been very heightened, emotionally charged, and tied to personal identity. When clients in my office decide to re-examine long-held beliefs related to reproduction, they sometimes find themselves in an anxious thought spiral: *If I give myself space to process how complicated this is, what if I change my mind? If I change my beliefs, will I find myself voting differently or advocating for things differently? Then what are other people going to think about me? What is God going to think about me? What am I going to think about myself?*

In reality, there is a lot of healing and clarity that comes through sitting in the complexity of life, especially when we do it alongside each other. The work of being with someone transcends career and vocational training; it's something we can do whether we're a therapist, doctor, pastor, accountant, dancer, or any other vocation. No matter how uncomfortable it may be, we can sit with other people through complex life experiences, because as humans, we have the ability to connect. We are at our best when we're practicing the art of being with each other.

---

*Ginny Lupka, LCPC, is a mental health counselor practicing in North Carolina, with a masters in counseling from Covenant Theological Seminary in St. Louis and a focus on reproductive mental health.*

# 6

# Resisting False Assumptions

YEARS AGO, A PASTOR TOLD ME, "The fire and brimstone way I used to preach about abortion was rooted in the thought that I couldn't understand how anyone could choose that. Now that I've heard the research and understand the emotional reality of shame, I can understand why."

When I dig deeper into responses to the abortion issue that feel off to me, I usually find there is a foundational assumption about the problem that doesn't line up with what I've learned through research and experience. If you've ever struggled with physical or emotional symptoms that took doctors a while to diagnose correctly, you likely understand how frustrating it is to listen to people give you advice when they aren't correctly assessing what is happening. Providing support, help, or solutions is impossible without a clear understanding of the problem.

Imagine if the church drew on our historical legacy of radical compassion and support and applied it in the context of abortion today.

Imagine us united—not in blaming those on the "other side" or misunderstanding people with lived experience—but in recognizing that the deeper issue is a narrative of shame.

Then, imagine leaning fully into the truth of grace, allowing it to reshape how we talk about abortion.

What might shift? First, the culture of our communities. Then, ultimately, our reputation.

And what could happen then? Picture someone navigating an unintended pregnancy, parenting alone, or processing an abortion, thinking

*I know Christians will be safe. It will be a relief to talk to someone at a church.* It's a big dream, but it has happened before—with Jesus and with many iterations of his church throughout history. People who felt they had nowhere else to go approached him. They cried out to him, interrupted him, cut holes in roofs, or reached out and touched him. This is our heritage.

## CONFUSING SELFISHNESS FOR SURVIVAL

Several months into leading the Christian pregnancy organization, I had a conversation with a woman who had been leading a similar organization for ten years. The stated mission of our organization at the time was to reduce the number of abortions. I found that many of our programs were based on assumptions about what women needed, not actual data, research, or conversations. I thought maybe she had done research or asked this question, so I asked her, "Why do you think women have abortions?" With a flat voice she simply replied, "Selfishness."

I had only been in the job for a little while, but I could already tell that wasn't what was happening for the women we served. I was hearing stories of women in such painful and difficult circumstances that when I imagined myself in their shoes, I could envision myself considering abortion. This is why listening to women's stories has been so pivotal in my personal journey of becoming prograce. The way things look to us from the outside can often be very different from the inner reality and the obstacles people face.

I was at a church leaders conference in Chicago recently, and a woman told me that in her urban neighborhood and church, she knew women who had multiple abortions and seemed to approach them casually. I asked if the women she knew had suffered any trauma in their lives, and she responded with an empathetic yes, that they had endured not just some trauma, but layers upon layers of trauma. She immediately made the connection that even though the women had an outward appearance of nonchalance, if she stopped to ask them questions, she would quickly discover connections between their trauma and the decisions they were making. There was so much more happening inwardly than she had assumed based on what she observed outwardly.

If we want to act more like Jesus in the abortion issue, we must understand what is at stake for a childbearing woman. The reason so many women see abortion as essential to our functioning as equal citizens in our society is because our society isn't equal when it comes to reproduction. Even though two people create a child, one person carries the child and most of the responsibility. For many women living in this society and deciding to have an abortion, *selfishness* doesn't even come close to describing what is happening. We know from research that *survival* is the more accurate word. Women make the decision to have an abortion because of their need to survive in a collectively broken world.

When we falsely assume the reasons women have abortions, it skews the way we think about women who have abortions as people. Often, but certainly not always, the program models and stated impact results of Christian abortion outreach efforts point to an underlying belief that we must "rescue" innocent children from women making poor choices. When we don't recognize the real drivers of abortion (shame and lack of support), we focus our efforts on discouraging women from choosing abortion. We make it about what is happening right now, in this short window of time a woman has to make this decision, rather than what she is experiencing on an ongoing basis from her long-term support system—her partner, family, church, or community.

## THE IMPACT OF OUR NARRATIVES

A couple in their late teens came into our pregnancy organization for help. His dad was a local pastor, and her family was also Christian. They told their counselor, "Our parents have told us, 'Don't ever come home pregnant.' So telling them is not an option." They decided on abortion—a first experience for her and a second for him. The counselor told me that in follow-up sessions, the young woman was overwhelmed by the experience and shut down emotionally, so she wasn't sure she could help her process the decision.

I have heard more similar stories than I can count about Christians having abortions alone, or only with their partner knowing, because they were terrified of what their parents would think of them. They talk about all they have heard about pregnancy and abortion growing up, and how they feel unable to bear the weight of a parent changing their view of them. As a parent myself, it caused me to evaluate how I communicate to my own kids that I want them to feel safe coming to me with anything, which was part of my journey to understanding that becoming more like Jesus really is the goal.

Christian outreach around abortion has historically placed a lot of emphasis on talking to a woman in the few weeks she has to make an abortion decision, with the implicit goal that Christians should seek *more* opportunities to have these influential conversations. And even Christians who aren't involved in direct outreach to women sometimes give priority to the question, "What should we say to a woman who is considering abortion?" The irony is that people making this decision don't come to Christians for support in the first place, because of what they have already heard from believers throughout their lives.

I don't know if the Christian parents of these teenagers actually said, "Don't come home pregnant" verbatim all those years ago. I often hear people joke that their parents used to say this, when really the message was communicated more implicitly and gradually. Regardless, these kids heard something that communicated to them that the impact of being pregnant—what it would do to their identity, to their parents view of them, to their future—made abortion feel like the best option.

This is not just true for Christians. It's a pervasive narrative in our culture and is well-illustrated by this scene in the 2007 movie *Juno*, when Juno tells her dad and stepmom that she's pregnant.

Juno's dad: I thought you were the kind of girl who knew when to say when.

Juno: (pause) I don't really know what kind of girl I am.

The scene then cuts to her dad and stepmom processing the pregnancy.

Juno's dad: Did you see that coming when she sat us down here?

Juno's stepmom: Yeah, but I was hoping she was expelled or into hard drugs.

Juno's dad: That was my first instinct, too, or a DWI. (pause) *Anything but this.*

"Anything but this" expresses the mental loop women tell us they can't get out of when they find out they're pregnant. They need a place to process the pregnancy without losing their identity or disappointing their parents. But if they have only heard from their parents that unintended pregnancy is devastating, or unacceptable; they often don't think their parents can provide what they need.

Several years ago, I was talking with a woman who primarily worked with churches that support legal abortions. What she was seeing was that women at these churches also didn't feel comfortable going to their church, because they heard nothing about unintended pregnancy or abortion beyond the occasional mention of the political stance. These churches had also underestimated the emotional needs pregnancy presents and hadn't gone beyond stating their legal views to demonstrate that they would be there for a woman if she needed them.

## MISUNDERSTANDING ADOPTION

When I started working at the Christian pregnancy organization, I found a brochure in our lobby focused on adoption from a national organization. As I flipped through it, I became increasingly uncomfortable with the messaging and statistics about what happens to children of single parents, including their rates of addiction, depression, and crime. Even though this happened twenty years ago, I remember the sinking feeling that this brochure from a credible organization was promoting the idea that if you parent your child alone, you are putting them at risk, so you should place them for adoption.

I got this same feeling in the years leading up to *Roe* being overturned when I would hear Christian leaders say something along the lines of, "Is the church really ready for *Roe* to be overturned? Are we ready to adopt all the children?"

These attitudes reflect the underlying assumption that we need to "rescue" children from parents with moral failures or who don't want children. In reality, nearly 60 percent of women who have abortions already have a child.[1] Caring for the needs of other children shows up in the top reasons women have abortions.

Because we've made wrong assumptions about who has abortions and why, we also misunderstand the reality of adoption. As we found in our research, an unintended pregnancy ushers in a "death of self." Another qualitative study took it a step further and examined the different kinds of death perceived in each of the three outcomes of an unintended pregnancy:[2] *Parenting* involves the death of the woman's identity; *abortion* involves the death of the potential relationship with the child; *adoption* involves the death of the woman's identity and the death of the potential relationship with the child. That is why it's often perceived as the more significant pain.

Years ago, at an adoption agency training session, I learned that most women don't consider adoption until the third trimester; they must first go through the process of accepting the "death" of their identity by deciding to parent. Then, some will consider adoption. But most still will find it too difficult to consider because, as a 2015 study describes, "Adoption was a decision that represented taking on, and then abdicating, the role of parent."[3]

Another top concern of women in the 2015 study was that adoption could put their child at risk if they were placed with an unsuitable adoptive family. Open adoption can alleviate much of this concern, but the concern is deeply ingrained in women. One woman, who didn't want an abortion but saw no other choice, sent a follow-up letter to our pregnancy organization; she outlined all the reasons why she couldn't have a child, then concluded with, "So I sent my child to heaven." This perspective was the only way she could think of solving the various "deaths" involved in an unintended pregnancy.

I believe adoption, particularly open adoption, can be a beautiful experience for children, birth parents, and adoptive parents. And the primary way I see this happening is by replacing the narrative of shame around unintended pregnancy, which leads to "death of self," with a narrative of grace and support.

Sitting with women's stories transforms our thinking, and that transformation will change not only the way we engage in conversations about this topic, but our posture and attitude in those conversations. When we sit with the reality women describe, we gradually start to understand that if we had been walking in their shoes, we might very well have done the same thing. This awareness moves us into a posture of humbly receiving grace for the assumptions we have made, and asking God to reframe our thinking.

## Always More to Someone's Story
*—Andrea Capuyan*

I was twenty-five years old and a Bible college graduate when I found myself in an unintended pregnancy. I was in shame upon shame upon shame. I tried to live for a long time in denial that I wasn't really pregnant. I had been having a lot of suicidal thoughts, wondering if I should kill myself.

It was roughly twenty-five weeks before I admitted the truth and knew that something would have to change. I picked up the phone and called a local pregnancy center, since I thought they provided help to people who were stuck in a pregnancy.

I said, "Hi, I'm pregnant. I want to place this baby for adoption, but I haven't seen a doctor. I don't know what to do. How can you help me?" The woman on the phone said, "We don't do medical care. You're going to have to go get Medicaid. That's going to be a long process. You'll have to wait all day in line to sign up for that."

When that phone call ended, I remember thinking that they didn't want to help me.

I felt really discouraged, thinking, "I just want to get this over with. How do I get out of this? I want this to be over." I went to the next listing in the phone book, which was Catholic Charities. I picked up the phone and gave them the same spiel: "Hi, I know I'm pregnant. I haven't seen a doctor at all, and I want to place my child for adoption. How can you help me?"

I don't know what else the woman on the phone said, but I remember hearing her say, "Oh, sweetie, we need to get you into care." Looking back, it could be that they both had ways to help, but I heard only obstacles from one person and an "Oh, sweetie" from the other.

Several years later, I was sitting in a room with other directors of pregnancy centers, talking about our services and sharing ideas. One of the leaders asked about perhaps expanding into providing some medical care. And another leader said, "You don't want to go down that road. That's not who you want to serve. Remember, we exist to help women not have abortions." And in that moment, I felt like I was right back on the telephone with that first phone call to a pregnancy center.

I remembered my conversation with the first pregnancy center I called when I was pregnant; I thought, *Oh, I did hear her right. I really wasn't who they wanted to help. They didn't want to help people who have already told them their plans. They only wanted to help people who might be choosing abortion, so they didn't want to help me.* The team at that pregnancy center didn't know that I genuinely was contemplating suicide. They didn't know the shame that I was in, that I was a Christian thinking *I just want to get this pregnancy over with, and then I am leaving the church. I'm leaving God behind. He is done with me, and I am done with him.* There was no way I was going to share that over the phone with anybody, because I was filled with shame. I would have needed to trust them to tell them.

That has a lot to do with why I lead the way I lead today. We do not know what is happening in the lives of people on the other side of the phone. They will tell us what they think is safe to say to us. The things that they believe will invite us to respond with a caring attitude so they might receive connection and compassion. So if we try to ascertain their intentions and persuade them, we are fooling ourselves and full of arrogance.

The father is now my husband. Even though I kept him out of the decision-making process for a long time, he supported me with the adoption decision I made. Even then, I was in a spiral of thinking, *If anybody finds out about this, I've ruined his life. I've ruined my life. I've ruined this baby's life. I've ruined everything.*

We went to a community birthing class together. One day, the instructor stopped the two of us and asked if she could talk to us for a second. She knew nothing about us. She had just been with us in class for about six weeks. And she said, "I just want to tell you, I watch couples in class. I don't say this often to couples, but

I just want to tell the two of you that you guys have this." I think of her often.

To simply hear somebody saying "I've been watching you, and you guys are going to make it" was stunning to us, and it was a seed of hope. She had no idea what depth of encouragement she was giving me at that moment. I suddenly felt like hope was not abandoned. *God has not abandoned me. We are going to survive this.*

*Andrea Capuyan is the executive director of Laurel Pregnancy Center in Laurel, Maryland.*

# 7

# Collective Versus Individual Responsibility

YEARS AGO, I GAVE THE KEYNOTE SPEECH at a benefit dinner for the pregnancy organization I was leading. At the time, I didn't have this ProGrace framework mapped out exactly like it is now. Still, every year, I would feel inspired to help our supporters understand the reality for women and why we needed a new way to think, talk, and engage around abortion.

That particular year, I was thinking about how many women among the audience of nine hundred would have had an abortion. I wanted to address them specifically, so I said something like, "Tonight, we see you. And I want you to know I'm sorry for any way the church or any Christians made you feel that you couldn't come to us for emotional or practical support. I hope you know you can come to us now."

One of my friends, a board member, pulled me aside afterward and said, "I'm not sure I'm comfortable with making a corporate apology for something we didn't individually do." Yet it seemed natural to me that I would take some ownership of how my larger faith community had responded to unintended pregnancy and abortion. I was immersed in research and women's stories, and I felt convicted that Christians had played a significant role in perpetuating narratives that lead to shame and isolation.

In the years since that particular instance happened, I've watched as this idea of taking collective responsibility has been translated as political and become divisive; but it doesn't have to be when we can look through the lens of the kingdom rather than partisan politics.

## THE EMPATHY OF JESUS

In Luke chapter 7 we read the following story:

> Soon afterward, Jesus went to a town called Nain, and his disciples and a large crowd went along with him. As he approached the town gate, a dead person was being carried out—the only son of his mother, and she was a widow. And a large crowd from the town was with her. When the Lord saw her, his heart went out to her and he said, "Don't cry."
>
> Then he went up and touched the bier they were carrying him on, and the bearers stood still. He said, "Young man, I say to you, get up!" The dead man sat up and began to talk, and Jesus gave him back to his mother.
>
> They were all filled with awe and praised God. "A great prophet has appeared among us," they said. "God has come to help his people." (Luke 7:11-16)

In the historical context of this story, a widow was among the lowest and most vulnerable, because without a husband to provide for her, she was destined for a life of poverty. Her son was the only link that would save her from destruction, as he was the one who could work and provide for her.

When this woman's son died, she likely experienced tremendous fear about her future along with the grief of losing him. She most likely would need to fight for her survival, but she didn't ask Jesus for help. Maybe she hadn't seen him yet or couldn't see him through her weeping and tears. Perhaps she was still in shock, so she couldn't do anything but put one foot in front of the other. We know that twenty-five of Jesus' pre-resurrection miracles happened after the person, their friends, or their loved ones asked him for help. This miracle is one of only twelve when no one asked for help. So why did Jesus stop for this woman?

First, he took the time to see her. The Greek word for "saw" in verse 13 is *horaō*. This word can mean to see with the eyes or to see with the mind (or know), to experience, and to care for. Whatever he saw of her and her precarious situation, his heart went out to her. The Greek word for "heart went out to her" in verse 13 is *splanchnizomai*, which means to be moved to one's bowels. At that time, the bowels were considered the seat of love and pity. As Bible Hub online describes, usage of this word "conveys a deep, visceral feeling of compassion or pity. It describes an emotional response that moves one to action. . . . It is frequently used to describe Jesus' response to the suffering and needs of others, highlighting his empathy and readiness to help." His empathy moved him to give her back her son. With that, he also gave her back her life.

Jesus didn't ask the woman if she had done anything to land herself in this predicament. He stopped, paid attention to what was happening to her, and was incredibly tender in his response. Jesus took it upon himself to perform a miracle for someone who was without protection in her society.

We find another description of the empathy of Jesus in Hebrews:

> For we do not have a high priest [Jesus] who is unable to empathize with our weaknesses, but we have one who has been tempted in every way, just as we are—yet he did not sin. (Hebrews 4:15)

The Greek word for "empathize" in verse 15 is *sympatheō,* which means "to be affected with the same feeling as another, to suffer with, to sympathize with, to feel for, have compassion on." It speaks to sharing in someone's suffering and, again quoting Bible Hub, "implies a deep emotional connection and understanding, going beyond mere pity to a heartfelt empathy that moves one to action or support." The Cambridge dictionary defines the word *empathy* as "the ability to share someone else's feelings or experiences by imagining what it would be like to be in that person's situation."

In recent years, as our culture has grown more polarized, I have encountered pushback from some Christians over the word *empathy*.

Their concern is that some people are misusing it to promote political agendas. But the fact that a concept can be co-opted or misapplied doesn't mean it should be dismissed.

*Empathy*—being moved by the reality of others—is not only grounded in Scripture, it's central to how Jesus engaged with the world. Time and again, we see him responding not with indifference or mere pity, but with compassion that leads to action. Empathy, then, is a defining aspect of God's heart. Whatever our political views, Christians are called to embody that same posture.

## PRESSURES TOO GREAT TO BEAR ALONE

When a person is facing external pressures too great to bear alone, do we share in collective responsibility? Isn't this why we provide for Americans through our welfare programs? Beginning in the 1930s, in the wake of the Great Depression, the US government created Social Security, public housing, and food programs to ensure protections for everyone in our country.[1] Though we may disagree on the specifics of welfare and food assistance programs, most of us can agree: We have some responsibility to care for one another. But when it comes to unintended pregnancy, that sense of shared responsibility often disappears. Society tends to frame it as a personal issue—something an individual or couple faces alone—with public debates focusing on whether a woman should have the legal right to terminate the pregnancy. Our language can suggest that every pregnant person begins on an equal playing field and is solely responsible for the outcome. In reality, the situations surrounding each pregnancy vary widely.

When we recognize the complex needs women face in the context of reproduction, it becomes clear that legal arguments alone won't resolve the issue of abortion. Instead, we're invited to ask a deeper question: In what way do we share a collective responsibility for the needs of those experiencing an unintended pregnancy?

## REALITIES OF UNINTENDED PREGNANCY
## IN OUR SOCIETY

To consider our collective societal responsibility, let's look at the factors that make abortion more likely. When approximately six in ten people who have abortions have already given birth to one or more children,[2] we have to think about how difficult it is for many people in our society to raise a child.

For starters, the financial realities of raising a child are staggering. Recent studies show that full-time working mothers are paid $0.74 to every $1.00 paid to fathers.[3] The United States doesn't regulate childcare costs, which continue to increase to the point that they have outpaced in-state college tuition in some states.[4] A conservative estimate is that childcare costs for one child are equal to 50 percent of monthly housing costs.[5] Our country ranks fortieth on a UNICEF ranking of forty-one high-income countries' childcare policies, while maintaining some of the highest childcare costs in the world. In 2022, New Mexico became the first and only state to make childcare free for families with demonstrated financial need.[6] The average US citizen also pays more in healthcare costs than most other nations, with medical debt being the leading cause of bankruptcy,[7] and single mothers pay more for healthcare than single fathers, married couples, or people with no children.[8]

Other systemic inequalities that make abortion more likely aren't as easy to quantify with data. They're often so deeply embedded in our culture that they go unspoken. The 2025 documentary *Prime Minister*, directed by Michelle Walshe and Lindsay Utz, profiles Jacinda Ardern, who became only the second world leader in history to give birth while in office. Her pregnancy sparked intense public debate as many people questioned whether she could—or should—continue leading New Zealand while raising a young child.

Other types of inequality also often go unnoticed. For example, if a male collegiate athlete is part of a pregnancy, does it impact

his scholarship or status on the team? What if it is a female athlete—
what would happen to her scholarship or status? If a man is
working toward a promotion at work, will that be in jeopardy if he
is part of a pregnancy? What would happen to a pregnant woman's
promotional progress?

We have been so conditioned to accept this inequality as natural
in our society that we don't even question it, but it is not God's design.
Pregnancy is a responsibility shared by two people, not just one, and
all people in society share a responsibility to care for each other, so
here is another area where Christians can ask new questions: How
can we advocate for pregnant women across professional and aca-
demic fields to protect them from life-altering consequences that
their male partners do not face?

## WHAT IS OUR RESPONSIBILITY?

Years ago, I met with a couple who generously supported our
Christian pregnancy organization. I shared stories about the needs
women expressed and how we were beginning to refer them to places
they could access practical support, such as registering for insurance
benefits, finding affordable health care, and career help. I thought
they were tracking with me through my presentation, and then the
husband responded. He told me that they owned a temp agency and
that his practice was to not hire pregnant women because he didn't
feel he could count on them to show up for the jobs—they were just
too unreliable.

I knew this couple cared about supporting pregnant women
through their financial partnership, so I was sad to learn they didn't
support pregnant women through their business practices. But I
was more sad about how his statement reflected the way many
Christians have focused on individual decisions while ignoring collective realities. One of our highest Christian values is to work for
justice for all people because we all have inherent dignity and worth.
This justice is one of the things we're asking God for every week

when we pray the Lord's Prayer in churches across the world: "Your kingdom come, your will be done, on earth as it is in heaven" (Matthew 6:10). If we commit to this kingdom vision in the context of the abortion debate, we assume collective responsibility to work toward making our society more equal between men and women, who share responsibility for the welfare of children. One way we can be faithful to our collective responsibility in regard to abortion is to honestly evaluate any ways we have absorbed or contributed to the cultural narrative that a woman facing an unintended pregnancy is "other" or "less than." Aligning our hearts with Jesus' to communicate dignity and grace is the first way we share in collective responsibility. From there, we start to see many more ways that we can live out our responsibility, implementing just practices in our spheres of influence.

We can ensure our churches, nonprofits, and Christian-owned businesses value pregnant and parenting employees, offering paid maternity leave and flexible working options. We can offer programs through our churches that benefit single parents—childcare, legal help, food pantry, and scholarships to church schools. We can advocate for policies and create programs that provide for pregnant women, single moms, and children. We can hold our government accountable to protect the interests of all people, not only those most economically valued.

## COLLECTIVE SUPPORT

When I found out I was pregnant with my son Noah, a week after accepting the position of executive director, it dawned on me that I would have to ask my board for maternity leave only nine months into my new role, and that I would want some flexibility once I returned as I co-parented an infant. I was so nervous to tell them that I waited until the last possible minute before it became too late to hide the pregnancy beneath baggy clothes. I remember feeling red blotches creep up my neck as I took a deep breath and told my new board that I was pregnant.

I was worried I was going to have to explain the years of struggling with infertility or tell them this was all God's fault because I had prayed to get pregnant before accepting the role. But I didn't have a moment to think of any defense, because they immediately launched into congratulations and excitement for me. It wasn't lost on them that my experience was so closely related to our mission. I took another deep breath and asked if they would grant me a thirty-two–hour work week for Noah's first year. They answered yes immediately and unanimously, and when I asked them why they were so sure, one of them replied, "We want you to lead this organization. We'll take you for however many hours we can get you."

My board's response was incredibly healing. I mattered. They wanted me. Their view of my gifts, capabilities, and leadership didn't shift because I would have a baby. And they didn't put up obstacles that would make it more difficult for me to continue to work while parenting the way I wanted. Quite the opposite: They respected me enough to grant my request of reduced hours. I remember thinking, "This is how it should be."

## COLLECTIVE RESPONSIBILITY

Through the last several election cycles, I've heard Christians express one of three primary options regarding their responsibility:

- To vote for the person or party who will make abortion illegal
- To vote for the person or party who will enact the most policies to help vulnerable people in the country across all social issues
- To vote for someone who will keep abortion legal and safe

These responsibilities involve legislation, so it makes sense to hear Christians discuss them in an election year. The problem is that they dominate our discussions even beyond national elections.

On both sides of the debate, we tend to be so focused on our political responsibilities around abortion that we minimize our Christian responsibility to value and protect people who experience pregnancy, which is an inherently vulnerable experience. But Scripture paints a clear picture for how we are to act toward people in vulnerable positions:

> Religion that God our Father accepts as pure and faultless is this: to look after orphans and widows in their distress and to keep oneself from being polluted by the world. (James 1:27)

> Suppose a brother or a sister is without clothes and daily food. If one of you says to them, "Go in peace; keep warm and well fed," but does nothing about their physical needs, what good is it? In the same way, faith by itself, if it is not accompanied by action, is dead. (James 2:15-17)

> If you see some brother or sister in need and have the means to do something about it but turn a cold shoulder and do nothing, what happens to God's love? It disappears. And you made it disappear. (1 John 3:17 MSG)

> Learn to do good. Seek justice. Help the oppressed. Defend the cause of orphans. Fight for the rights of widows. (Isaiah 1:17 NLT)

> Whoever oppresses the poor shows contempt for their Maker, but whoever is kind to the needy honors God. (Proverbs 14:31)

> All they asked was that we should continue to remember the poor, the very thing I [Paul] had been eager to do all along. (Galatians 2:10)

Why haven't we collectively applied these Scriptures in our response to abortion and responsibility to women facing unintended pregnancy?

Maybe generations before us honestly didn't know how to help women, since judgment and shame were so prevalent; women were often taken away by their religious families to a maternity home to deliver and then place their child for adoption, whether that was what they wanted or not. The experiences and needs of women were likely even more mystified and misunderstood than they are now. Perhaps the church didn't know how many women lacked the emotional and practical support needed to have a child, but now we do know. We now have a plethora of data that tell us why women often feel like abortion is their only option. Not all of their answers relate to being materially poor, but many do. And all of their needs fit into these Scriptures, which tell us how we are to care for others when they are in need.

What would it take for the church to collectively apply those Scriptures now? We can start with the example of Jesus in John 8 that we looked at in chapter two. The Pharisees came to him asking him to focus on the sin of the woman, but he didn't. Jesus focused on the collective sins of those with power, rather than accommodate their request to condemn the most vulnerable person. He did this time and time again in his life.

If we hold this example up against the US church's collective response to abortion, it becomes painfully apparent that, while so much of the Christian narrative has been about an individual or couple's abortion decision, we have mostly ignored the collective brokenness we are *all* a part of. In doing so, we have blamed vulnerable people for systemic fractures we share collective responsibility to heal. While a woman ultimately makes the decision to carry or terminate a pregnancy (sometimes in collaboration with her partner), it is collective brokenness that creates a narrative of shame, places inordinate responsibility on the woman, and limits her options.

For example, we accept as normal the reality that women will bear most of the financial responsibility for a child if the man doesn't pay child support. We put so much emphasis on our vote to make abortion legal or illegal, but we often don't emphasize the other laws we vote on that could make child support, medical care, childcare, and job protection financially accessible to every pregnant woman. We also don't focus on the power we already have to shift the narrative in our sphere of influence, as my board did for me. How we speak in our families, workplaces, churches, and communities matters.

People often ask me what the outcome would be if the church took collective responsibility and improved the systemic and cultural conditions that contribute to abortion. This is a question I can't answer for sure, and I continue to be primarily motivated by our shared responsibility to reflect the image of Jesus, but I have some thoughts of what *could* happen.

From everything I've seen in research and experience and conversations with people with lived experience, I imagine we would see more hope, more possibilities, more empowerment, and more thriving. We would be helping pregnant women, and we would also be meeting the needs of vulnerable people on a broad scale—children, families, communities. Supporting pregnant women and correcting these societal inequalities is a place Christians can find common ground and unite to make a significant difference. It's a more holistic, kingdom way of evaluating our ethical responsibility and the outcomes.

### Using Language Shaped by God's Kingdom
#### —Katie Potts

My first pregnancy was not a planned pregnancy. I was married, employed, twenty-seven years old, and had done everything "right" according to my conservative Catholic upbringing, but I still felt ashamed to go buy a pregnancy test. I had a massive support network and a husband to parent with, and still I thought, "I don't know if I can do this."

You don't realize, until you've done it yourself, the toll pregnancy takes on a woman mentally, emotionally, and physically. It comprehensively changes you. I gave up so many of the things I wanted in order to be pregnant and give birth. The first four months of my daughter's life, I openly told people, "I want her to go back to where she was. I want my old life back."

For a long time, I called myself a pro-choice Christian, and that often brought up cognitive dissonance for the people I spoke to. I didn't have language to communicate my belief that all life is sacred and we live in a fallen world where women are not actually experiencing what we would consider a choice. If I'm not communicating what I want to be communicating, then I need to find new language. ProGrace has done that for me and helps me to better express the fullness of what I believe.

The terms *pro-life* and *pro-choice* have become so twisted and laden with stereotypes that we need new language to describe what we truly believe. Presenting myself as a prograce Christian calms the waters so that I can have conversations that aren't laced with stereotypes with people who differ from me politically. Saying I am prograce means that, first and foremost, I value both women and children equally, and also that I empathize with the insurmountable challenges many women are facing.

I believe that in an ideal world—in God's kingdom—a woman wouldn't have to make this kind of choice, because there would be systems set up to support her. If we do want to reduce abortions, the pathway is to give the woman the support she says she needs, whether it's emotional, financial, or babysitting so she can go to school. Whatever support we can provide as the church is what's going to make the difference in her life.

It's not my end goal, as the person supporting her, to influence her decision. She is the person in front of me with a need, and I am the Christian there, committed to supporting a person in front of me with a need. Giving her what she needs, regardless of what decision she makes, is what I believe Jesus calls us to do. This is what I see Jesus doing for others throughout the gospels.

No words can fully express the vision of God's kingdom, but ProGrace language helps me avoid fighting and division with Christians who are different from me, and instead have conversations that point toward this shared vision.

---

*Katie Potts is a former educator who has worked for ProGrace since 2022. She and her family are active members of the United Methodist Church.*

# 8

# Looking Back
# to Move Forward

In an effort to understand the current state of Christian engagement in the abortion debate, I've done some personal research on historic Christian outreach around unintended pregnancy. The vast majority of this mobilization has been outside the parameters of local churches, and since I view local churches as one of the primary expressions of how God's kingdom comes on earth, I wanted to know why. I keep the history fairly general here, because it's challenging to find unbiased information; most articles I have found are written by people with strong partisan affiliations, both pro-life and pro-choice. I have included a few links in the notes from both sides if you would like to read more.[1]

## CHRISTIAN OUTREACH—PREGNANCY CENTERS

In 1967, a Catholic man founded the first Christian pregnancy center in Hawaii after abortion was legalized in that state. When *Roe v. Wade* was passed in 1973, the American Catholic church was firmly against the ruling, while other denominations had a mixed response. Many Christian groups chose to advocate politically, and others began offering direct support to women facing unintended pregnancy. By the early 1980s, the movement for churches—and even denominations—to launch self-standing, independent pregnancy centers was gaining momentum. Various pro-life and pro-choice websites list the number of pregnancy centers in the United States and Canada today at anywhere between 2,500 and 3,000. Most of these are independent nonprofit organizations that were started by Catholics, Lutherans, or evangelicals.

Though most Christians don't work directly with pregnancy centers, it's important for all of us to examine this model for several reasons. First, we need to understand why churches chose to focus their outreach to pregnant women outside the church, because that perception still impacts how we view our role as a faith community today. Second, these organizations were founded by Christians, so their practices are an outward demonstration of deeply held Christian mental models and assumptions about abortion. As such, they offer each of us an opportunity to look inward and evaluate if we share any of these perspectives. And last, because there are so many existing direct service organizations today, they could be key partners in the church's collective efforts to have a Christlike response to abortion if both the organizations and the churches are willing to look inward and examine their historical mindsets and practices.

## WHY THIS MODEL

Why did Christians establish independent pregnancy centers instead of building support programs within local churches? From both research and conversations, I consistently hear two main reasons. First, many believed that women considering abortion were unlikely to seek help from a church. Second, they felt that churches lacked the capacity to offer the specialized care women might need.

Today, most pregnancy centers provide services such as pregnancy tests and ultrasounds, with some offering broader support like prenatal care or mental health counseling. This marks a shift from earlier decades, when centers typically focused on administering pregnancy tests and facilitating a discussion with volunteer advocates—many of whom had little to no medical or social service training. Medical, mental health, and case management services were not the original motivation for creating these organizations. The primary goal was to create neutral, non-church spaces where women facing unintended pregnancies would feel safe and comfortable seeking help.

The perception that women and men avoid churches when considering abortion still holds true today. However, we now have a clearer understanding of why. It's not due to anti-religious sentiment, discomfort with church settings, or unfounded concerns about Christians. Rather, it stems from a fear of judgment and a belief that Christians are not reliable sources of support. While the pregnancy center model responded to a visible need—offering an alternative to churches for those facing unintended pregnancies—it didn't address the root issue. That deeper problem exists within the church itself.

## LOOKING INWARD VERSUS DEFENSIVENESS

I participated in a nonprofit conference at North Park University during my first year leading a Christian pregnancy organization. I was still working on my common ground–elevator pitch, but most people who heard it assumed I was politically pro-life. A woman from another nonprofit started questioning the efficacy and professionalism of one of our programs, and I could feel the heat rising in my face. Earlier in the conversation, she had used a word that I associated with a pro-choice affiliation, so I made the leap to assuming she was pro-choice. Because of the stereotypes I had of pro-choice people at the time, I also assumed she was comfortable with any and all abortions.

I replied to her with an unprofessional level of irritation and said, "Well, we know what your perspective is on abortion." She took a breath and replied very evenly, "No, you don't know what my perspective on abortion is."

She was right, I didn't know her, nor did I ask her any of her perspectives on the issue. I felt shame when she questioned our program, and I lashed out in defensiveness to deflect the shame somewhere else.

In the early days of my leadership at the pregnancy organization, my colleague and I drove to the suburbs to attend a group of eleven

Chicago area pregnancy center leaders who met regularly. Before one particular meeting, in which the group was going to discuss pooling our resources to advertise together on Moody Radio, I printed an article about pregnancy center practices from a well-known, pro-choice website. I was becoming concerned about certain practices as I immersed myself in the stories of women who visited Christian pregnancy centers.

The practices listed in the article can still be found in more recent publications like the American Medical Association Journal of Ethics.[2] They included:

- Failing to disclose the services they provide, so that some women are surprised to find that the organization doesn't provide abortions or refer to abortion clinics

- Using words like "counselor" for volunteers or staff who don't have professional counseling accreditation

- Training staff to persuade women toward parenting and adoption while stating on their website that they offer unbiased exploration of all pregnancy options

- Referring to medical studies from biased and incredible sources that exaggerate the medical and emotional risks of abortion

I held up the article I had printed and said, "Before we join together in this project to advertise on the radio, I want to confirm that none of our organizations engage in any of these practices."

Knowing what I know now, I wouldn't have used a pro-choice publication to raise my concerns with this group. But at the time, I was focused on the content, not the source. "People are saying these things about Christians serving women facing unintended pregnancy. Don't we all want to ensure there is no truth in any of these accusations?" I expected a simple and nonpolitical affirmation of common ground. So, just like at my high school reunion, I felt shocked by the silence around the table. One of the leaders finally said this wasn't pertinent to our discussion about the radio partnership, and they moved on.

As a result of what I brought up that day, the leadership of this group told me they were concerned that I was taking my organization in a pro-choice direction. As a nonprofit leader, I understand how challenging it can be to have someone raise concerns that you don't expect or agree with, so I understand some level of their initial defensiveness. The group never did answer my questions, so I didn't know what their practices were, and my team and I decided to not partner with them on the radio partnership.

## HISTORIC PRACTICES

When I arrived at the Christian pregnancy organization, it was over twenty years old. We offered ultrasounds and some of our advocates were licensed and trained counselors, but specialized medical or mental care was not our priority internally. The archived training materials I discovered confirmed what I heard from the staff and volunteers. Our staff had been trained and evaluated based on two primary goals:

- Talk a woman out of an abortion
- Share the verbal gospel with her

While trying to understand our service model, I sat in on a session with one of our clients, facilitated by one of our team members who had her masters in counseling. The client wasn't married, already had two children, and shared that she was already struggling to manage life. She couldn't imagine parenting another child. Instead of asking questions to discern what needs the woman had and explore how she could connect her to support, my colleague responded with a lengthy encouragement on why the woman should consider adoption.

As a licensed counselor, my colleague had been trained to use a question-based approach and let her clients' needs lead each session.

However, because her job performance was measured by whether or not a woman changed her mind about abortion, she went against her training and used a persuasion-based approach.

Prioritizing sharing the gospel and talking a woman out of an abortion at a pregnancy center reveals fundamental assumptions about women who are considering abortion. We assume she is not a Christian, that she doesn't understand pregnancy or fetal development, and that she isn't thinking about the welfare of the child. These assumptions lead us to educate, inform, or try to emotionally persuade a woman away from abortion, because we believe she needs to be redirected. Though most of us will never speak directly to a woman considering abortion, if we share these fundamental assumptions, they will leak out in our conversations and influence the culture of our families and churches.

Though dissuading from abortion and sharing the gospel were our internal priorities, these were not disclosed publicly on the website nor in any conversations with the women we served. When I began leading, the organization had two websites. The website for clients stated women would receive unbiased information about all their options and unconditional support from nonjudgmental counselors. Nowhere did it disclose we were a faith-based organization. The separate website for donors was filled with pictures of newborns and images of baby feet. It described the organization's impact through statistics of "babies saved" from abortion and women who received Christ.

As our team learned more, through the research we commissioned, about the reality of what is happening for people with this lived experience, we began to rethink our existing mental models. It helped to ask: When we are in struggle and in a similar state of panic, isolation, and shame that an unintended pregnancy initiates, what have we found to be Christlike and helpful from others?

When our leadership team shifted the practices to a listening-based model led by the client's need and permission, one of our colleagues in particular wrestled with the change. She resisted the new practice out of fear she may only have one chance to talk to a woman before an abortion decision. A few months later, she spoke up at a staff meeting about an experience she had with a counselor who only used Bible verses to answer every issue she brought up instead of letting her vent or process her feelings. She didn't feel seen or heard and was leaving each session frustrated. Then she told us she sensed the still, small voice of God saying that her clients felt the same way when she gave information instead of listening and meeting them where they are at.

After that day, I watched her perspective on interacting with clients change permanently. But I think I was changed even more than she was. I realized I had also tried to persuade her to adopt the practices I was passionate about—even as I was telling her not to try to persuade others! This was a pivotal point in truly coming to understand that God's ways are higher than my ways.

Throughout the process of reforming our approach, our team encountered God in powerful ways as we trusted him to lead our counseling sessions. We hired only professional counselors to work with women. Even with their training, they shared it could sometimes be challenging to let the client lead the session and not tell her what to do.

One counselor shared her experience of meeting with a young woman who stated she wanted an abortion and then directly asked, "What do you think God thinks about this?"

My colleague took a deep breath and asked God what to say. Immediately, a question popped into her mind, and she asked the client, "You told me earlier that you believe in God. What do you think he is saying to you?"

She said the woman sat still for a second, then her countenance changed. She said, "Right when you said that, all the ways God has been there for me in the past flashed through my mind. And then I realized he will be there for me if I continue this pregnancy."

Grace, active listening, and asking questions are never a means to an end to persuade someone to our way of thinking, but rather a respectful way to communicate that we value someone enough to listen. It's an empowering form of communication. When someone has to stop and think about a question, they own the answer much more than if we try to tell them something. Jesus is the master of this approach; we see him use it repeatedly in the Gospels. Not only does the Spirit reveal truth to us, he can reveal it to others. But this is God's responsibility, not ours. Even when Jesus used this approach, some people walked away from him; he gave them that choice. We can't control outcomes for others. When we try, we risk being distracted from our own journey toward Christlike character, and we may inadvertently resort to persuasion or manipulation—paths that are never in line with his teachings. This is true whether we work in direct service, church leadership, or simply are trying to discern how to talk about abortion with our friends and family.

## LOOKING FORWARD

Even though most Christians aren't involved in direct service to women considering abortion, the belief about our responsibility to persuade others permeates US church culture. This belief may take different forms depending on the faith tradition, but there is a consistent trend of being outward-focused rather than inward-focused. The direct service outreach models I have experienced came out of evangelical churches, and they directly reflect mental models that still exist today. I often hear church members ask, "What should I say to a woman considering abortion?" Not because they will interact with a pregnant woman within the short window of time she has to make a decision—most of us won't—but because they have been told their responsibility is to be ready to say something at this time.

Even if our specific denomination doesn't communicate this message, the question of what is or isn't our responsibility regarding abortion is one all Christians should consider.

As Christians, we can agree that we share the following responsibilities:

- Honor the inherent dignity and *imago Dei* in every person
- Wrestle with the mystery of pregnancy and God's creation of life
- Care collectively for people in vulnerable situations
- Show compassion and grace to fellow believers in a conversation often marked by judgment and blame

Focusing on these shared responsibilities opens the door for Christians with diverse perspectives to move forward in unity—especially where we have historically avoided conversation or collaboration.

We can further reflect on our responsibility to Christlikeness by asking these questions:

- How have I developed my mental models and attitudes around abortion, and how can I better align those with the ministry of Jesus?
- What does my language and posture communicate, and how can I become safer for this conversation?
- What do I know about the realities for people navigating this experience, and how can I better understand and empathize with them?

These questions are especially important for individuals involved in direct service to pregnant women. Unfortunately, I know of some organizations that still have similar practices to the ones I listed in my group meeting twenty years ago. These practices continue to do damage, not only to the women receiving services, but also to the well-intentioned people trained in those models. However, there are many Christian pregnancy organizations across the United States and Canada today that provide professional, ethical, and invaluable support. I am encouraged as I network with leaders who have been asking these questions for many years and building programs that dignify and empower women as a result. I've seen God move in these organizations when they maintain a nonpolitical approach, listen to women, and provide support without an agenda. This is true for the pregnancy organizations that are a part of our Equip learning community, and I'm grateful for those leaders who are using the ProGrace approach to communicate what is already in their heart to align their organizations.

The thousands of pregnancy organizations today have enormous potential for positive impact. Most of them were founded by churches, but many now see congregational support for their mission waning as divisiveness increases, and as a result they face challenges such as lack of funding and lack of volunteer help. Not only will they need resources, but they will need to partner with institutions, such as churches and social service agencies, to help facilitate long-term support systems for women if we are really to see the change we long for.

My hope is that the common language of a prograce approach will serve to connect like-minded leaders, staff, and volunteers from various organizations and churches so they can collaborate, building powerful partnerships to serve as the hands and feet of Jesus in our communities. This is also an opportunity for Christians to address the limits of this historic outreach model existing primarily outside of local churches—coming full circle as pregnancy organizations and churches unite to focus on the internal condition of the church and becoming more like Jesus.

## Heart Change Happens Through Listening
### —Tiffany DelHousaye

Hope Women's Center provides safe haven for at-risk women and girls facing any difficult life situation, so though it's not the primary focus of our work, serving women with unintended pregnancies is a significant part of what we do. When we had conversations with women about their pregnancies, we often felt tension between our identity as a Christian organization who believes in life at conception and our desire to meet their very real needs. Then we found ProGrace, and we thought, *This is it!*

ProGrace language has been a powerful tool for us, not only when serving women with unintended pregnancies, but every woman facing a difficult situation. Anchoring our practices in a ProGrace approach has helped us communicate what was already in our heart—a desire to serve women in need. We don't tell women what to do; we ask questions. We emphasize her options, giving her space to process what she wants and take ownership of her situation. It's amazing how this empowerment transforms not only a woman's present situation but her life in general going forward.

Since being trained in the ProGrace approach, Hope has trained several great churches in our area. The people we train have been relieved and excited to have tools that help them communicate their heart in non-divisive ways. It can take time for the message to really set in, and sometimes people will say, *This is great, now will you join us for a pro-life march this weekend?* We graciously decline to participate in marches; the main reason is that marches often contribute to cultural narratives of shame for women who've experienced abortion. I do my best to be understanding in these conversations, remembering I had similar thoughts before working with ProGrace, even though my heart was always to serve women. There were things I said and did that I hadn't realized would be interpreted in the way they were.

God changed my heart through the stories of the women I listened to. Hearing women share their experiences, I've come to understand where they're coming from when they make the decisions they do. I understand why they stayed with their abuser. I understand why they terminated their pregnancy. Once I humbled myself and became teachable, I started to understand things that I thought I had figured out before.

If someone's hurting, it doesn't feel good to hear Christians saying "It's your fault." Instead, we can start by agreeing with the fact that they are hurting. Then we can humbly consider if we are complicit in anything that contributes to their hurting. And then we can ask how we can contribute to their healing.

When I read the Gospels, Jesus always meets the need first. He heals first, he feeds first, then he teaches. My hope for the church is that when people come to us in need, we will be able to stop, listen, and prayerfully respond. This doesn't mean there's not going to be friction and pain. Abortion is a complicated topic, and sometimes we will have to agree to disagree, but we do not need to divide a church or break fellowship with a friend because we have a different perspective. No matter what we believe about the morality of abortion, we as Christians can be the hands and feet of Jesus by listening and responding without judgment to the needs other people present us with.

---

*Tiffany DelHousaye is director of operations at Hope Women's Center, a nonprofit with multiple locations in Arizona.*

# PART 3

# Reforming Paradigms About Women

# 9

# Reframing Motherhood

I HAVE HAD TWO COMPLICATED pregnancies and deliveries. I lost so much blood after Noah was born that I couldn't physically do much for the first two weeks. I remember crying at the dining room table, feeling overwhelmed and hopeless, thinking of all he needed and how little I had to give at that moment. And this was a child I had waited ten years for! I still felt like myself with many hopes for my own life and his, but I was at a standstill for those early weeks because I had given everything I had. I couldn't think about dreams; all I could do was recover. In those moments, a thought took hold: "I feel this way at thirty-eight with a lot of family, community, and financial support. What if I were eighteen, alone, and had no support?"

## MOTHERHOOD VERSUS A WOMAN'S DREAMS

My husband committed to my dreams of leading the pregnancy organization and secured special permission from his employer to work from home one day a week to be with Noah, which was uncommon in 2007. Additionally, my board granted me a thirty-two–hour work week, which included two days from home.

While work flexibility is increasing in many fields, these types of accommodations aren't guaranteed by the US government, and they are still at the employer's discretion. Throughout many fields of work in our culture, we see rigid standards that present obstacles for mothers and pregnant women to advance or even maintain employment. In many cases, these obstacles are peripheral to the work itself—meaning the quality of the work would not be directly jeopardized by more flexible policies to accommodate parenting. With more women in the workforce than ever before, we're becoming painfully aware of how few legal safeguards are in place for pregnant women and parents of young children.

This reality is accepted in many of the legal arguments around abortion. In the 1992 Supreme Court case *Planned Parenthood of Southeastern Pa. v. Casey*, the majority Court opinion stated, "The ability of women to participate equally in the economic and social life of the Nation has been facilitated by their ability to control their reproductive lives."[1] In 2016, to argue against the undue burden of abortion access in Texas, 112 women in the legal profession who had also had abortions filed an amicus brief with the Supreme Court. They began the summary of their argument by stating, "To the world, I am an attorney who had an abortion, and, to myself, I am an attorney because I had an abortion." Their argument includes evidence that access to abortion directly impacts educational opportunities and is critical for career advancement in their field.[2] Additionally, their brief cites a study from 2011 that examines the effects of the timing of motherhood on women's career paths, finding that delaying motherhood leads to an increase in earnings of 9 percent per year of delay.[3]

More than three decades of research reveal a consistent pattern: Women's earnings decline with each child they have. The drop is steeper when a woman changes employers, suggesting a discriminatory tendency to stereotype mothers in the workplace. In contrast, men can see their wages rise by 3 to 10 percent after becoming fathers.

These patterns are known as the *Motherhood Penalty* and the *Fatherhood Premium*. While researchers continue to explore the complex factors driving these trends, the data is clear: "As a result of the wage penalty associated with motherhood and the wage premium tied to fatherhood, the gender pay gap widens as men and women move through the life course. Parenthood is therefore a key contributor to gender inequality."[4]

Many Americans accept these challenges to motherhood as normal. This inequality reveals a deeply rooted societal narrative—one that has shaped our collective thinking to the point that we no longer recognize it as injustice. The church in the United States has a unique opportunity and responsibility to present alternative values that honor parenting alongside careers. We can't overlook the realities these statistics represent and the narrative they have created: You must sacrifice your dreams to have a child. What is God calling us to do in response to this narrative?

## WHEN MOTHERHOOD DOESN'T HAPPEN LIKE IT "SHOULD"

Sarabeth was born three years into our marriage, which was considered normal in our community at the time. By the time she was about seven, I could predict how conversations introducing my family were going to go:

"And this is our daughter, Sarabeth."

"Oh, you just have the one?"

"Yes."

(pause) "Are you going to have any more?"

I often told strangers more than I wanted to about my reproductive challenges, then I fumed all the way home about their perceived insensitivity and my own lack of boundaries. Even if I had not chosen to disclose as much, the questions alone would still have bothered me. I loved our family of three and didn't feel we were incomplete.

And yet, the questions seemed to indicate we were missing something or doing something wrong by not having another child. I now know those questions were based in the same frameworks that can make us insensitive to the realities of unintended pregnancy. If we don't examine the unconscious standards we may have for how we think families should look, we can easily miss the emotional pain around pregnancy.

*We're used to families looking a certain way.* When we had a three-person family, people in my sphere seemed to adhere to an unspoken norm that people should have at least two kids but no more than five, otherwise they are a bit odd. A woman participating in the ProGrace workshop told me that the research about panic and shame around an unintended pregnancy took her back to her experience of an unexpected pregnancy with her fifth child. She felt embarrassed to tell people, and when she did, some commented, "You know how to prevent that, right?"

During the workshop, she came to understand that she had experienced shame when people in her church community put their expectation of a reproductive story onto her in this way. And yet, she hadn't even been able to articulate it until she heard the research. We sometimes don't realize how strong a narrative like this is because it's embedded in our culture.

*We don't have a framework for understanding emotional pain around pregnancy.* I imagine the people who asked me about only having one child did not expect it would cause any pain. Well intended as they may have been, this is based on an assumption that pregnancy should happen right when we want it to—not before and not after. So if I didn't have a second child, people reasoned it must have been by choice. They thought it was an odd choice, so they asked me about it, and I often interpreted that to mean I was somehow different or odd.

This sense of "should" around pregnancy compounds the pain and sense of isolation women experience around infertility. I've often wondered why I didn't disclose to very many people that we really did want a second child. I wouldn't even have thought to use the words *secondary infertility* until many years later. At the time, we really didn't have a framework for talking about sadness around pregnancy. When it didn't work out the way we thought it would, we didn't know how to bring it up with others or respond when they brought it up to us.

This same sense of "should" also compounds the pain and sense of isolation women experience around unintended pregnancy. One of the women we served at the pregnancy organization told me that she was pregnant and single at the same time her sister was pregnant and married; her family threw a baby shower for her sister but not for her.

When we better understand the complexities and challenges women experience in pregnancy—whether intended or not—we can broaden the abortion conversation from its one-dimensional focus on whether or not abortion should be legal. We can take it to a more comprehensive discussion that honors motherhood and all reproductive stories in the many forms they take.

## RISKS OF PREGNANCY

Both sides of our debate focus on the moment of decision while failing to attend to the emotional impact pregnancy has on women, regardless of decision.

The emotional weight of pregnancy had not even been considered in medical research until just recently. Death by suicide accounts for 20 percent of deaths during pregnancy and the first year after birth, making it one of the leading causes of maternal mortality, as reported in a government study from 2022, but this type of reporting is very recent.[5] The authors explain, "While there is robust data surrounding medical conditions such as postpartum hemorrhage or hypertension as they relate to maternal mortality, research surrounding suicide and maternal mortality has been relatively limited. This is partly because until recently, deaths related to behavioral health were not considered to be pregnancy-related, and not counted toward maternal mortality rates." The fact that researchers didn't even track deaths related to behavioral health in pregnant and postpartum women points to a cultural narrative that pregnancy is simply medical and biological, without taking into account the full impact it can have on a woman.

A 2019 study published in the *American Journal of Obstetrics & Gynecology* came to a similar conclusion when researching the broader category of self-harm.

> The rates of maternal death secondary to self-harm, including suicide and overdose, have been omitted from published rates of maternal mortality, despite growing attention to the prevalence of perinatal mood disorders. . . . Underlying psychiatric disorder, including depression, is consistently identified as a risk factor in substance abuse and suicide. . . . Pregnancy does not protect against these risks, and the postpartum period has been identified as a particularly vulnerable time. The lack of consistent and inclusive data on self-harm deaths in the pregnancy-postpartum period is alarming.[6]

Pregnancy can also carry more physical risks than we commonly think or talk about. A few years ago, I was having a conversation for our podcast with some new friends in New York City. One of the women was pregnant, and she was feeling paralyzed by fear, trying to choose an OB/GYN and hospital for the baby's delivery. I hadn't experienced that type of anxiety around pregnancy medical care, so I asked her why. That's when I first learned how high maternal mortality rates are for African American women.

Currently, Black women are three times more likely to die from a pregnancy-related cause than White women.[7] A 2020 research project reported,

> More recent studies have shown that social factors such as historical exposure to racial trauma, discrimination, and marginalization; systemic barriers such as systematic racism and implicit bias within the healthcare system; the possibility of being uninsured; reduced access to reproductive healthcare services; and socioeconomic factors also contribute to pregnancy complications for Black women and have to be given consideration.

These social determinants of health show that poor maternal outcomes for Black individuals are caused by factors of racism that are embedded in healthcare and affect marginalized groups of individuals disproportionately.[8]

The more I learned, the more embarrassed I was that I had never heard of this disparity. Over decades of working in this field, I have listened to many people talk about high abortion rates among women of color, leading them to open pregnancy centers in minority communities, but I have never heard one of those leaders mourn or even mention disproportionately high maternal mortality rates in those communities.[9]

In 2024, the Associated Press reported on the completion of the first study to offer a detailed map of a woman's brain throughout pregnancy and two years after birth.[10] One particular quote from the study's coauthor stood out to me: "There is so much about the neurobiology of pregnancy that we don't understand yet, and it's not because women are too complicated. It's not because pregnancy is some Gordian knot. It's a byproduct of the fact that biomedical sciences have historically ignored women's health."

As Christians, we can have no part in discriminating against pregnancy, minimizing how strong women need to be to walk through it, or flippantly disregarding the physical risks women assume. As a people who believe God creates all life, we should champion the well-being of both the woman and the child—not just during the pregnancy but also after.

## MOTHERHOOD AND FATHERHOOD TOGETHER

In all four bodies of our Emotional Inquiry® research, the researchers point out that only a tiny percentage of women say anything about their partner when they recount their emotional experience. The women generally discuss their story as if they got pregnant alone. Even if they can later articulate that he was supportive or if they are still together, her initial and immediate perception is that she is alone with the experience, alone with the decision, and alone with the responsibility.

This subconscious omission points to an intense cultural narrative that we hold women more responsible in parenthood than men. Thankfully, the idea that a woman cannot work outside the home and be a good mom is becoming less pervasive, but moms are still held to a higher standard than dads when it comes to a child's welfare. We often frame it as societal honor and respect—and though it can be, it's a double-edged sword that can be burdensome for many women. That burden isn't healthy for women, children, or men.

We can honor parenthood, families, and God's design for life so much more when we communicate the following:

- Mothers and fathers are equally important and equally responsible for the welfare of their children.

- Mothers and fathers are equally important in their gifts, dreams, and desires to contribute to society.

- Because women carry a child for nine months and in many cases nurse for many months after, they need extra accommodation, support, and protection in those early years of parenthood.

## OUR RESPONSE TO ABORTION FLOWS FROM OUR VIEW OF WOMEN

For a long time, I saw abortion as a separate issue from gender issues in the church. I thought I could just stay concerned with abortion and help people align around a theological framework that empathizes with the experience of unintended pregnancy. But the church's historical response to abortion is directly connected to our historical view and treatment of women. The ways we've normalized misogyny and objectification and repeatedly dismissed women's concerns are at the root of why we've developed an approach to abortion that needs to be transformed.

To truly communicate a value for all human life, we must reframe our view of reproduction to include the complications, risks, and needs that come with it. Christians can unite in honoring the fact that God's design of pregnancy affirms the goodness of our human interdependence. With that interdependence also comes vulnerability and risk, for all humans, and especially for pregnant women. While women assume the emotional weight and physical risks of pregnancy in a unique way, it doesn't mean they are meant to do that alone. All people will ultimately suffer if we don't share in the vulnerability of reproduction.

Distorted paradigms about women are a primary root of the abortion problem as it exists today. Think about it: In a society with true equality, no woman would be left to navigate a pregnancy—conceived by two people—on her own. She would not face the loss of employment, financial advancement, or educational opportunities because of pregnancy. Men would share equal responsibility for both pregnancy and parenting. And countless women who do not desire abortion, but feel they have no other viable option, would finally have the genuine choice they deserve. I don't hold out much hope for our society in general to look this way, but I do dare to dream that the church of Jesus could.

## The Church Women Deserve
### —*Vivian Long*

When I read the statistics about how many women come to church for counsel or support with an unintended pregnancy, it saddened me, but didn't surprise me. It didn't surprise me because in my own life, when I was dating my (now) husband, who was not a Christian at the time, I didn't want to go to a church for counsel on the relationship. I thought, "I already know what they're going to say. There isn't going to be a dialogue." The church has increasingly become seen as a place where it's not encouraged to have a dialogue, where you're going to get an answer, and more likely than not, you're going to know what that answer is before they say it.

Churches have traditionally been places where people in crisis can go for care, safety, and mercy. In Los Angeles, churches are providing support to people who lost homes in the fires, and it's not controversial. No church is debating whether or not they should help. But for some reason, we look at women in crisis very differently. There are *many* debates between Christians over whether or not we should help them at all. So many of the messages we've heard from the church about abortion stem from the question, "What do women in crisis deserve?"

A prograce approach first and foremost reorients us to see women the way Jesus sees them—deserving of love, care, and understanding.

After *Roe v. Wade* was overturned, I wrestled with having to choose between identifying as pro-choice or pro-life. For most of my twenties, I aligned more with a pro-choice way of thinking: I wasn't a proponent of abortion, but I fully support individuals having the autonomy to make their own decisions about their body. I would now say that I have better language to articulate my views on abortion as aligning neither with the pro-choice nor pro-life movements, but stemming from a place of deep grace for women experiencing unintended pregnancy. I believe God grieves when people have abortions; I don't think that's God's intention for us. But I also believe God grieves when we mistreat each other and fail to see each other with the value he's bestowed on us. It grieves God whenever we exploit people, whenever we take advantage of the vulnerable, whenever we let pride, greed, or envy take over our hearts.

A Christian value for life cannot start and end with the topic of abortion. Imagine how much more honoring to families it would be if we advocated *for* women experiencing infertility, miscarriage, or stillbirth instead of advocating *against* women considering abortion. Imagine if the church got behind things like paid maternal leave or universal healthcare; these seem like radical ideas, but they would tangibly make it so much easier for moms to have thriving families. Instead, we have largely chosen to put our might behind something punitive, something that is designed to punish women, particularly those that are already the most underserved. This is not how Jesus responded to people in crisis.

ProGrace language has been a tremendous help for me in communicating convictions that I can stand behind, that don't conflict with my Christian beliefs, but actually are an expression of them. I need a prograce approach in my day-to-day conversations, and not just related to this issue of abortion. I need it as a mom, and I think a lot of other moms need it. In this context, having a prograce approach means building trusting and loving relationships that allow other moms to feel like they're seen and heard.

My heart's cry for the church is not only that seven out of seven women would come to the church to have a conversation about their abortion decision, but seven out of seven women would be supported by the church when they make their decision, regardless of what that decision is. And if that decision includes them becoming a mom and having children, that the church will truly be a partner with them in that journey. This process is what Jesus calls us into, not the outcome. The outcome is God's alone.

---

*Vivian Long is executive director of the Long Family Foundation and lives with her family in a suburb of Los Angeles.*

# 10

# Reforming Sexual Myths

LET'S REVISIT THE STORY IN JOHN 8:1-11. Why do most Bible translations call this story "The adulterous woman"? Why isn't it instead titled "Pharisees misuse and weaponize the Law"? Or "Religious leaders use a woman"? Or—incredibly relevant to our day—"Jesus protects a woman from clergy abuse"? We have been so conditioned to focus on the woman's adulterous behavior as the point of the story that we don't highlight the gross sin her religious leaders committed against her.

Even if it wasn't a set up by the Pharisees and she was willingly engaging in adultery, they abused their power by singling her out, putting her alone in front of a crowd, and insisting that the law demanded she alone be stoned when it did not. We know Jesus saw their wrongdoing for what it was, because he used the situation to protect a woman and correct church leaders' sin against her.

After bringing the woman before Jesus and the crowd, the Pharisees start by saying, "Teacher, this woman was caught in adultery, in the very act" (John 8:4 NASB 1995). The Greek word for "caught" is *katalambanō*, which means "to lay hold of, to seize upon." So yes, this means exactly what it sounds like in English. If they are telling the truth, she was engaged in a sexual act, and they laid hold of her right there, which brings up an interesting point—who else was there when they grabbed her in the act and dragged her to Jesus? A man.

So they tell Jesus a half-truth. They did lay hold of the woman, but she wasn't engaged in adultery alone. Even before they brought the woman to Jesus, they wronged her. There were two people in the sexual act right in front of them. They spotlight the woman for public judgment—alone—without bringing the man into public exposure.

They then tell another half-truth when they say, "In the Law Moses commanded us to stone such women" (John 8:5). That's not the entire truth of what the Law says. Consider these passages:

> If a man commits adultery with another man's wife—with the wife of his neighbor—both the adulterer and the adulteress are to be put to death. (Leviticus 20:10)

> If a man is found sleeping with another man's wife, both the man who slept with her and the woman must die. (Deuteronomy 22:22)

The Law clearly states that both the man *and* woman should die. So even before the religious leaders brought the woman to Jesus, they twisted the Law for their own purpose. Then, they dared to misquote Scripture to the Son of God and expect him not to notice.

Oh, he noticed. It gives me comfort and encouragement that Jesus noticed, and he went right to the heart of where this started. It didn't start with the woman; the Pharisees thought this up and instigated it. They were comfortable with a woman receiving a death sentence, alone and in clear violation of the Law. Why?

The Scripture tells us, "They were using this question as a trap" (John 8:6). Their purpose was to trap Jesus, and it didn't seem to matter to them what happened to the woman. It's easier to casually think a life is expendable if you have been dehumanizing and objectifying that category of people your entire life.

So Jesus starts with their wrongdoing, not hers. And here is where this story highlights a similarity with today's Christian hypocrisy regarding unintended pregnancy and abortion. We point the finger at the woman and accuse her of casually thinking the life of a child is expendable; all the while, we're still dehumanizing and objectifying women in the church. We need the grace and truth of Jesus to correct any bias we have toward women, and specifically women facing unintended pregnancy.

Eventually, everyone there with Jesus gets the opportunity to experience transformation. The woman is transformed. The religious leaders are given a chance to be honest about the errors in their own lives and acknowledge their need for Jesus. The crowd has the opportunity for transformation as they see the grace and truth Jesus extends to both the woman and the Pharisees. But the one person who might miss the opportunity for transformation is the man who was committing adultery, if he didn't follow the Pharisees out as they dragged the woman to Jesus. If he stayed hidden in the dark, ashamed of his part in this plot, he would be the one person in the story who missed encountering Jesus.

## CONSEQUENCES OF NORMALIZING OBJECTIFICATION

In my Protestant tradition, we are hearing story after story of Christian leaders objectifying and abusing women. Some of these leaders are men I have had personal or professional connections to, so these revelations hit me especially hard.

In 2018, I read in the magazine *Christianity Today* that Pastor Bill Hybels had resigned after ten women had accused him of sexual misconduct and abuse of power.[1] I respected Hybels and his ministry values. The church he founded, Willow Creek Community Church, was a close partner with our pregnancy organization for ten years, during the time this misconduct was happening, though we weren't aware of any of the accusations. I had thought for years that if I could just meet Hybels and help him understand the work we were doing, he would love it, and Willow Creek could be a good place for women facing unintended pregnancy to find support.

In full disclosure, I also thought his visibility could help my organization achieve our vision through greater exposure and connections. So I tried to secure a meeting with him several times. I was uncomfortable with a few things I had heard him say about relationships between women and men over the years, but I pushed down my concerns because "he could help our good cause." When the news about his misconduct eventually came out, I felt deflated and disillusioned. I had tied so much importance to pursuing a man to promote a ministry for women facing the vulnerability of pregnancy—not realizing that man was exploiting the vulnerability of women. As similar events continued to happen over the next several years, my sense of disillusionment grew.

In 2021, I read that Christian apologist Ravi Zacharias had been systematically abusing women for more than a decade, although the news was only made public by *Christianity Today* and *Religion News* after his death in 2020.[2] Before I started working at the pregnancy organization, he had been the keynote speaker for the annual benefit dinner. Zacharias was invited to speak so he could use his specialty in apologetics to state why abortion was wrong and to convince people it was a worthwhile investment to donate to the work. He was chosen to promote a ministry serving women, and he accepted this invitation and others like it for similar organizations. Thousands of Christians listened to his teaching on how to address abortion, and yet all along, he was acting in direct opposition to God's heart toward women.

Finally, in 2024, I read in *Religion News* that Mike Bickle, the founder of the International House of Prayer (IHOP), had committed clergy sexual abuse with numerous women, including teens as young as fourteen, over several decades.[3] In 2003, I'd visited IHOP for a conference where I had a profound experience with the love of God that changed the trajectory of my life. The night I returned home, I had a dream that has continued to guide me in the work I do today. What happened at IHOP shaped me, shaped my calling to fight for women, and is now part of my story. And all along, the founder and head pastor had been abusing women.

As late as 2018, Willow Creek elders and attorneys were actively trying to silence women who spoke up about Bill Hybels's inappropriate behavior.[4] The board of Ravi Zacharias's ministry wrote an open letter in 2021, repenting and asking forgiveness from one of his victims for their refusal to believe her testimony in 2017.[5] In 2024, the former pastor of Gateway Church, Robert Morris, stepped down after admitting he had sexual relations with a twelve-year old girl in the 1980s. The victim then made public that she first told the Gateway Church elder board about this abuse in 2005.[6] When we see elder boards knowingly silencing women to protect their male leaders or calling a pastor's sexual interaction with a minor a "moral failure" instead of a crime, it points to underlying belief systems and brokenness that must be very deep and very old.

The problem isn't only the secret sin of leaders but also patterns of relating to women that some Christian men openly express and normalize. Beth Moore wrote this story in an open letter to men in 2018:

> About a year ago I had an opportunity to meet a theologian I'd long respected. I'd read virtually every book he'd written. I'd looked so forward to getting to share a meal with him and talk theology. The instant I met him, he looked me up and down, smiled approvingly and said, "You are better looking than _____." He didn't leave it blank. He filled it in with the name of another woman Bible teacher.[7]

I had a similar experience when teaching a ProGrace workshop hosted by a local pregnancy organization in another city. An older man who was a former leader with that center pulled me aside during a break and made an inappropriate comment about what I was wearing and his response to it. I was so shocked I asked the host of the event if this man had dementia. She responded, "No, he doesn't, why do you ask?" I told her what he said and how I thought surely he couldn't be in his right mind. She said no, that sounded like him. He had been a leader in the field of Christians supporting pregnant women for decades by this point.

Halee Gray Scott has done research with female and male Christian leaders for years. She has reached what she calls a "data saturation point"; she has heard so many stories of male/female work relationships in Christian ministry that are fraught with problems and mistrust because of hyper-sexualization.[8]

In all these examples, not only are the women sisters in Christ, but peers in Christian leadership. Sexualized comments from male colleagues diminish women's self-esteem and confidence in ministry, even though they have nothing to do with the woman. The comments reflect the heart of the man who speaks them—a man who is teaching others.

We also know that when misogynistic messages are so pervasive for so long, both women and men can internalize those messages. In my first year leading the Christian pregnancy organization, I heard a counselor describe her session with a young woman who wasn't married and had just discovered she was pregnant. Instead of expressing empathy or asking the woman what she needed, she told us she had talked to her about practicing abstinence. She said she asked the woman why she would want to "lie like a rug" with just any guy and get herself into this situation. This female counselor was participating in the narrative that the woman was morally flawed and solely to blame for the pregnancy.

With these attitudes present in Christian spaces, we shouldn't be surprised that we are now seeing increasing numbers of young women who do not feel safe in church. A 2024 study found that 65 percent of Gen Z women say churches don't treat women and men equally. That same study shows that young women who are disaffiliating from faith now outnumber young men.[9] And other research asked those who grew up in religious households why they left their faith and are now "nones." When they could select multiple reasons,

42 percent said religious hypocrisy, 31 percent said religious bigotry, and 28 percent said the harm caused by religion in the greater world.[10]

I don't get disillusioned by one leader having a "moral failure," because I know individuals are human and have broken, hidden patterns. But I begin to feel unsafe in the church when that leader is reinstated in ministry without adequate examination regarding whether any abuse of power was involved or going through the process of restoration described in Scripture. I feel completely unsafe when the leader's attorney frightens a victim into silence. I lose all confidence when elder boards ignore the concerns of women and conceal the injustice, and sometimes a crime. While I've had so many healthy and positive interactions with Christian men in leadership positions, the sheer number of these other stories of abuse can cause me to despair. How long have women been routinely abused in the American church? How many more women will have our trust broken before we see radical change?

We are living in a time when God is so active in revealing truth it makes our heads spin. One thing these experiences have done is build my faith that God is at work, even when I can't see it. If God is actively revealing this truth on such a public scale, we can have confidence that a new way is possible. We can take this opportunity, not just to call out and convict outward perpetrators who lead large ministries, but to ask God to reveal the deeper, hidden attitudes and mental models behind the actions, which often exist within us as well.

## DECONSTRUCTING SEXUAL MYTHS

I thought I had fully renounced the harmful messages I heard about women growing up in church, and then I read *The Great Sex Rescue* and *She Deserves Better* by Sheila Wray Gregoire, Rebecca Gregoire Lindenbach, and Joanna Sawatsky. As the authors held myths about sex up against the Word of God, I was surprised how much they still impacted me. The following are two myths they identify.

Myth One:

All men are in an unwinnable battle with lust, and women tempt them toward lust, so every woman who presents a temptation must be controlled.

Myth Two:

A woman is the guardian of sex in the relationship because men can't control themselves.

These myths stand in gross opposition to the equality and responsibility championed in the New Testament, yet they have been part of Western culture for hundreds of years and have taken deep root in the American church. They have directly impacted the way the church has wrongly treated women and handled issues like abortion, and they have been deeply harmful to men as well. The story that men can't control themselves, are doomed to be enslaved by lust, and will be tempted to take advantage of women is a degrading view of men, especially when we hold it up to Jesus, the ideal man.

In looking at the response of both Mike Bickle and Robert Morris, as well as other Christian leaders who have been accused of assault or abuse of a minor, I see a tendency among several of them to confess and then label it a *"mutual* moral failure."[11] This language indicates a desire to point blame toward the woman for what happened, even when the leaders were very clearly abusing their power and exploiting vulnerability. It's not a mutual moral failure when the woman is a minor or being groomed by her pastor; this is a lie rooted in the harmful belief that women are temptresses responsible for safeguarding the sexuality of both parties.

Harmful sexual myths are not only at the root of why men blame women for sexual abuse or pregnancy, but why women blame themselves. We see throughout research that women often believe they alone are at fault for a pregnancy, even though their partner had equal responsibility for the conception. When we see someone internalizing a discriminatory narrative against themselves, it points to a strong historical, cultural narrative that is so ingrained they don't even recognize it—that unintended pregnancy is the woman's fault. We have ingested the myth that "boys will be boys," but a woman should have known better.

How do we undo these myths in a Christian community? We can start by holding both genders equally accountable to the standard Jesus set for all humanity. The way to do that is to reorient ourselves around the belief that we are a family of equals.

## FAMILY OF GOD

The idea that men and women would share inheritance equally as adopted sons and daughters of God was unprecedented in the first century. And yet, early in Mark's gospel, Jesus introduces the idea, saying, "Whoever does God's will is my brother and sister" (Mark 3:35). We then see the apostles adopt this language throughout the New Testament, most often as the Greek word *adelphos*, which in the plural form is an expression commonly used for brothers and sisters, sometimes translated "brethren" or simply "brothers" in different Bible translations.

Acts alone has eleven references to Christ's followers as "brothers and sisters." Paul continues addressing and describing believers this way, beginning in Romans and continuing through the epistles. We then see the author of Hebrews continue this, as does James. Then John uses it repeatedly in his letter and even several times in Revelation.

I had no idea this language was so prevalent until I looked up every occurrence. Here are a few of my favorites to inform how God intends us to relate to each other:

> You, my brothers and sisters, were called to be free. But do not use your freedom to indulge the flesh; rather, serve one another humbly in love. (Galatians 5:13)

> And that in this matter no one should wrong or take advantage of a brother or sister. (1 Thessalonians 4:6)

Keep on loving one another as brothers and sisters. (Hebrews 13:1)

Finally, brothers and sisters, rejoice! Strive for full restoration, encourage one another, be of one mind, live in peace. And the God of love and peace will be with you. (2 Corinthians 13:11)

This is how we know what love is: Jesus Christ laid down his life for us. And we ought to lay down our lives for our brothers and sisters. (1 John 3:16)

Not only do we have this relationship with each other, but by some mystery we are also brothers and sisters with God's firstborn son: "For God knew his people in advance, and he chose them to become like his Son, so that his Son would be the firstborn among many brothers and sisters" (Romans 8:29 NLT).

That last passage illustrates the concept Amy Peeler outlined at the end of chapter one, that the incarnation is God's demonstration of equality, and it's combined with the theology that we are all God's children, male and female alike. It's a doubly radical idea: "And that's the way it was with us before Christ came. We were like children; we were slaves to the basic spiritual principles of this world. But when the right time came, God sent his Son, born of a woman, subject to the law. God sent him to buy freedom for us who were slaves to the law, so that he could adopt us as his very own children" (Galatians 4:3-5 NLT).

The family language in the New Testament makes clear that our relationship as brothers and sisters comes before any other societal norms for how women and men relate regarding relationships, sexuality, or reproduction. I know Christian men and women can relate as brothers and sisters because I have seen it—in my experience in the Vineyard church, in my working relationships with the boards of both nonprofits I have led, and in the way I see men and women relate to each other in the ProGrace community.

I met one pastor who was very open about his journey. He sensed God speaking to him decades after his college girlfriend's abortion.

He believed God wanted him to repent for being passive and not offering support, so he repented. He shared about his experience with abortion at a ProGrace workshop, which is where I first heard his story.

After the workshop, he trained a group of people at his church in the ProGrace approach. Around that time, a young single mom who had been attending the church became pregnant again. She faced pregnancy discrimination at her workplace, getting less than her usual number of hours. Then her partner walked away from her because she didn't terminate the pregnancy. This pastor was moved by her experience, and the church partnered with their local pregnancy organization to offer continued support. Her pregnancy was high risk, so together they made sure she had access to health care, and they checked in on her regularly. When she wasn't able to make her monthly rent because of the decreased hours at work, the pastor mobilized his congregation to cover her rent. The church hosted a large baby shower for her, gifting her with everything from diapers to clothes to gift cards. He sent me pictures of her dedicating her child at the church. We kept in touch, and a few years later, he told me that she comes to church off and on when it works with her schedule. Her life is complicated, but that is still her church family. He and his church are so grateful to be in her life and continue supporting her where possible.

All of this positive impact that the pastor has been able to initiate started with a private decision to let God into an experience he had locked away, and then to be vulnerable with his community. I'm inspired by his courage, compassion, and Christlike leadership, treating this young woman as a sister in need, not someone to be feared or judged. God is blessing her, her children, the members of the church who support her—and this pastor. He radiates peace and joy when he talks about his journey. I am inspired by his story and by other Christian leaders who are working to create similar expressions of grace in their faith communities. This is grace and truth in action. This is the way forward.

Grace allows us to sit with the question: What does it feel like to be a woman in the church when it comes to issues of gender, sexuality, and reproduction? Grace paves the way for us to be honest and intentional, evaluating whether our churches are safe for women the way Jesus was. I continue to learn that grace is essential for healing in the abortion conversation for all of us.

At the same time, extending grace doesn't mean excusing harmful attitudes or behaviors toward women. We can uphold accountability and consequences, protect and advocate for those who've been abused or exploited—and still extend God's grace to those who have caused harm. Everyone has worth in God's eyes, regardless of their actions. And ultimately, there is no true healing without grace.

Even in light of the many negative experiences I've had as a woman in church, I believe God's intention is for Christian spaces to be the safest community for women in our society.

Jesus is the ultimate defender of women. The way he treated women in the Gospels was radical for his era. If the early church could continue that legacy and elevate women to the status of co-leaders well above the standards of their society, then we can find a way to elevate women beyond the unjust norms of our own society.

## Grace for All
### —Rev. Dr. Darice Wright

We can make changes to legislation, but they won't stick unless there's a heart change. On one of the most transformative nights of my life, I stayed up most of the night crying, realizing that all of my irritation in social justice work, all of my wrath and stridency, didn't move us anywhere. It might've changed some things, but it didn't change things forever. It didn't change people's hearts, and that was the difference I was really looking for.

For my doctoral thesis, I wanted to help pastors fulfill their calling as shepherds when it came to issues of racism. My cohort was a group of white pastors from majority-white evangelical churches. I knew that while many of them weren't personally racist, they weren't actively working against racism or discipling their congregation to work against racism. I am an African American, ordained female reverend, so I knew I would need grace in order to have this conversation.

As I prepared, I thought about what we learn in seminary about internalized racism—when people who are the victims of discrimination begin to expect it, internalize it, and therefore treat themselves or each other a certain way. And I realized the flip side of that is internalized supremacy. You can't have one without the other. Internalized white supremacy is in the DNA of the United States. If, by legislation, my ancestors were told they are three-fifths human, and you're told you're five-fifths human, obviously you're going to think you're superior to me. Five-fifths trumps three-fifths all day long.

Before the first session, I wept like a baby, thinking, *Lord, I don't want to hear this.* It was incredibly difficult for me to agree with this notion of having grace for horrible actions. It sent me through the wringer. But then the thought came: How can you condemn someone for believing they're superior when that's what they've been told?

The hardest thing about starting conversations about internalized supremacy is the immediate erection of walls—"You are accusing me of white supremacy"—and I've learned that my job is not to plow through those walls, but to understand the dynamics at play for the person who puts them up. When we are able to understand those dynamics, then we can have empathy for someone who's impacted by internalized supremacy because of our country's history, just as we have grace and empathy for someone who is impacted by internalized racism.

Taking a ProGrace approach to these conversations, for me, meant saying, "I understand supremacy; how could you and your congregants not feel some of this, because it's in the DNA of the United States?"

The whole Christian movement has been centered on grace. It can't move forward without grace, which is maybe why we're stagnant when it comes to some of these justice issues. If you look at abortion or the way women are treated in regard to motherhood, the same principle applies. Men have been told that women are secondary, that part of showing up like a man in society involves having a woman be subservient. Men whose thoughts or actions align with these cultural messages are equally deserving of grace.

Because it's not about picking sides or thinking God is on my side. It's about me being on God's side. And God is clear about his side. While we were sinners, Christ died for us. It's the whole redemptive work of God clothing himself in humanity to step into earth, or as Eugene Peterson says in *The Message*, to move into our neighborhood. It's the grace message, period.

---

*Rev. Dr. Darice Wright is an ordained minister, preacher, and teacher who serves in the Chicagoland area and is developing a ministry of antiracism pastoral care as part of her doctoral work.*

# 11

# Reframing Women's Equality

MY EVALUATION OF HARMFUL PARADIGMS about women up until this point has been based on a rock-solid belief that men and women are equal image-bearers of God. This is a belief that all Christians agree on at a fundamental level. Though there is disagreement about how gender equality should be lived out in our society and churches—particularly concerning leadership and pastoral roles—I will not address those points of disagreement because I am speaking to the shared Christian value of human dignity. Because our understanding of human dignity has so much bearing on the way we think about abortion, it is important that we look again to the life of Jesus to understand God's nature in regard to gender.

If we agree on the dignity of all human life, then why do we need to emphasize this idea of equality? Because of inequality. To understand what Jesus revealed to us in his life about God's view of women, we must first understand the context of inequality in which he lived.

Women's stories don't normally appear in ancient literature from this time, due to cultural norms of men holding most positions of power, so it can be challenging to determine women's experiences and voices in those societies.

In her book *The Samaritan Woman's Story*, Caryn A. Reeder helps us understand how to approach writing from this time: "Across the Roman Empire, including among Jews and Samaritans, women of all legal, social, and economic classes were marginalized in various ways. Laws restricted their rights with respect to property ownership, marriage, and divorce. . . . In literary sources, we see women portrayed from the perspective of men. . . . These factors limit our knowledge of the lives and perspectives of women in the first century." She encourages us therefore to "proceed with caution through reconstruction of women's lives in the first century, aware of all that we simply cannot know—and aware of the ways the sources we do have may mask the complexities of women's experiences."[1]

With Jesus' arrival in the gospels, demonstrating how God acts in the world, we start to observe an unprecedented elevation of women compared to other literary examples from the ancient world. According to Jennifer Powell McNutt, professor of theology and history at Wheaton College, "Sometimes something can be so out of place that it draws our attention. By this principle, every time Scripture names a woman or includes a woman as an exemplar, we should pay attention. Scripture surprises us by going against the grain of its context."[2]

## REVEALING TRUTH TO WOMEN

In the society of Jesus and the early church, women didn't usually receive formal education or learn from male teachers. They did not sit *at the feet* of a rabbi, a term that was commonly used to denote a discipleship relationship. Paul uses this idiom when he says, "I am a Jew . . . educated at the feet of Gamaliel according to the strict manner of the law of our fathers, being zealous for God as all of you are this day" (Act 22:3 ESV).

In Jesus' ministry as a rabbi, however, he entrusted deep theological truths to many women. We even see the idiom "at the feet" used to describe a woman's discipleship to Jesus: "Now as they were traveling along, He entered a village; and a woman named Martha welcomed Him into her home. And she had a sister called Mary, who was also seated at the Lord's feet, and was listening to His word" (Luke 10:38-39 NASB).

Jesus returns to Martha and Mary's house after their brother Lazarus dies, and he says to Martha, "I am the resurrection and the life. The one who believes in me will live, even though they die; and whoever lives by believing in me will never die. Do you believe this?" (John 11:25-26). Jesus' proclamation that he is "the resurrection and the life" is pivotal and foundational to the Christian faith, and he makes this statement only one time—to a woman.

Martha responds, "Yes, Lord; I believe that you are the Messiah, the Son of God, who is to come into the world" (John 11:27). With her response, Martha becomes the third person to confess Jesus as the Son of God before his resurrection, joining Nathanael (John 1:49) and Peter (Matthew 16:16).

Jesus not only revealed theological insights to women who were his friends, such as Martha and Mary; when he encountered a Samaritan woman at a well, he had a lengthy interaction. He shared foundational and life-changing truths with her that apply to all his followers, male and female:

> Jesus answered, "Everyone who drinks this water will be thirsty again, but whoever drinks the water I give them will never thirst. Indeed, the water I give them will become in them a spring of water welling up to eternal life. . . . Yet a time is coming and has now come when the true worshipers will worship the Father in the Spirit and in truth, for they are the kind of worshipers the Father seeks. . . ." The woman said, "I know that Messiah" (called Christ) "is coming. When he comes, he will explain everything to us." Then Jesus declared, "I, the one speaking to you—I am he." (John 4:13-26)

Jesus doesn't just share one truth, but flows in conversation with her and weaves in several aspects of the Gospel and the kingdom of God. Both the length and level of interaction recorded in this conversation stand out. Jesus makes a statement, and she responds with an intelligent question; he answers her question, and they go back and forth like this six times.

In *The Samaritan Woman's Story*, Reeder describes in more detail why this conversation is so notable:

The Samaritan woman is a real partner in the discussion. Her responses and questions indicate her awareness of history, theology, and current events. She is insightful. In response, Jesus clearly announces the changing identity of the people of God— no longer Jew or Samaritan, but something else. And he clearly announces his own identity as Messiah. . . . She then testifies to his identity in her hometown. . . . Her neighbors listen to her! Because of her words, they follow her back to the well to meet Jesus for themselves.[3]

In this story, we see the immediate fruit of this encounter. She immediately communicates this truth to others and does it so convincingly that they come to the well to meet Jesus. And ultimately, "Many of the Samaritans from that town believed in him *because of the woman's testimony*" (John 4:39, emphasis added). She multiplied the truth Jesus entrusted to her.

## INVITING FEMALE FOLLOWERS

In addition to his twelve male disciples, we read in the Gospels and Acts about the women Jesus invited to follow him:

> Soon afterward, Jesus began going around from one city and village to another, preaching and proclaiming the good news of the kingdom of God. The twelve [disciples] were with Him, and also some women who had been healed of evil spirits and diseases: Mary, called Magdalene [from the city of Magdala in Galilee], from whom seven demons had come out, and Joanna, the wife of Chuza, Herod's household steward, and Susanna, and many others who were contributing to their support out of their private means [as was the custom for a rabbi's disciples]. (Luke 8:1-3 AMP)

Three of the women's names are mentioned, which was uncommon in ancient literature and would have stood out to the original readers. We also see women named elsewhere in the Gospels (a total of six) along with "many others" who had followed Jesus in Galilee, accompanied him to Jerusalem at the time of his arrest, and witnessed his resurrection (Matthew 27:55-56; Mark 15:40-41; Luke 24:10).

While we don't know how many women are included in the "many others," we see women present in the account of the disciples waiting for the Holy Spirit after Jesus' ascension. This indicates they were among Jesus' inner circle, along with his mother and siblings:

> When they arrived, they went upstairs to the room where they were staying. Those present were Peter, John, James and Andrew; Philip and Thomas, Bartholomew and Matthew; James son of Alphaeus and Simon the Zealot, and Judas son of James. They all joined together constantly in prayer, along with the women and Mary the mother of Jesus, and with his brothers. (Acts 1:13-14)

These followers of Jesus stayed together until the day of Pentecost, when women and men alike were filled with the Holy Spirit. Then in his sermon immediately following that event, Peter quotes from the prophet Joel and makes it clear what God's vision for the church is:

> In the last days, God says,
>    I will pour out my Spirit on all people.
> Your sons and daughters will prophesy,
>    your young men will see visions,
>    your old men will dream dreams.
> Even on my servants, both men and women,
>    I will pour out my Spirit in those days,
>    and they will prophesy. (Acts 2:17-18)

## VALIDATING FEMALE WITNESS

In the story of the resurrection of Jesus, each of the four Gospel accounts tells us women heard the news first, and all four mention Mary Magdalene by name (Matthew 28:1-10; Mark 16:1-10; Luke 24:1-12; John 20:1-18). I had heard this often talked about at Easter, but never heard that these women were devoted followers who had been traveling with him for years, along with the male disciples.

I had also heard that Jesus appearing to a woman first was a significant statement about elevating the value of women, yet I didn't fully understand the significance of this encounter until reading *The Mary We Forgot* by Jennifer Powell McNutt:

> Not only does Jesus call [Mary] by name, she was also the first person called by him after the opening of the tomb. Her calling was followed by a commissioning, which she received directly from Christ himself so that she became the first person (or among the first group of people) to be sent by Jesus to share the good news: "Go and tell." . . . We see her there as the firstfruits of a new priesthood at the very dawning of the new creation forged in Christ that is no longer exclusively Levitical and no longer exclusively male . . . no longer rooted in a person's traits but in a person's union with the Son of God.[4]

McNutt goes on to say that this encounter qualifies Mary to be considered the first apostle based on "the highest biblical definitions given in Scripture for apostolicity: (1) she accompanied the Twelve in Christ's ministry, (2) witnessed his death and resurrection, and (3) was 'sent' on a divine mission (Luke 10:3; Acts 1:21; 1 Corinthians 9:1-2; 15)."

Biblical scholars agree that God doesn't act in random or haphazard ways. A careful reading of Scripture reveals order and patterns that give insight into God's redemptive dream for his creation, which includes his interactions with women. What does this pattern mean for us in our current cultural moment?

## GUARDING THE EXAMPLE OF JESUS

It is not enough for Christians to say that Jesus elevated women in a way that was countercultural for his time. We must actively guard his example and seek to do the same in our time.

Jesus said, "If anyone loves me, he will keep my word, and my Father will love him, and we will come to him and make our home with him" (John 14:23 ESV). The Greek for "word" here is *logos*, which could also be used to describe the divine reason or plan. John illustrates this when he uses *logos* to describe Jesus himself as the Word, "full of grace and truth" (John 1:14). When Jesus says those who love him will keep his *logos*, he is talking about his full divine expression, flowing out of him through his actions and attitudes, as well as his words.

The Greek word for the phrase "he will keep" is *tēreō*, which means to keep intact, to guard, to watch over. It conveys the idea of watching over something attentively, to keep from loss or injury, observing it with the intent to preserve. To keep Jesus' word is not only to follow his commandments or avoid behaviors he spoke against. It is to attentively preserve, guard, and maintain in its original state the story of Jesus' life in all its expression.

This includes the stories he told, the way he acted toward people deemed below him in society, the cultural norms he broke, the religious traditions he challenged, the miracles he performed, the commandments he gave—all of it. When we combine the understanding of both *logos* and *tereo* in light of the life Jesus lived, which demonstrated God's view that every human is made in his divine image, we understand our responsibility as his church to model that expression and protect it from the inequality and dehumanization that too often surrounds us.

Modeling his expression means more than simply speaking or teaching about how Jesus elevated women. We must actively guard his example by demonstrating the same value in our culture.

Just as Jesus represented the Father through not only words but also his actions, attitudes, and relationships, we represent Jesus by how we treat individuals made in God's image. We can't model the full expression of Jesus if we maintain mental models of gender discrimination.

## REPRODUCTION AND EQUALITY

The apostle Paul wrote to the Corinthians, illustrating the interdependence and equality of the genders through the lens of reproduction: "But among the Lord's people, women are not independent of men, and men are not independent of women. For although the first woman came from man, every other man was born from a woman, and everything comes from God" (1 Corinthians 11:11-12 NLT).

In contrast, both sides of the abortion debate present reproduction as a problem that divides women from men. Abortion itself is a concession to the systemic inequities that women face when they are pregnant and parenting, especially when they are single, though the concession is also present for married women.

The first time the US Supreme Court ruled on behalf of a woman in a sex discrimination case was 1971 in *Reed* v. *Reed*. At that time, there were hundreds of state and federal laws that stipulated different rights and privileges based on gender alone, not to mention the lack of provision that was commonplace for women who were pregnant or parenting. Abortion then became legal in the United States in 1973, when there were still numerous laws that included discrimination on the basis of gender, not to mention all the commonly accepted practices of discrimination ranging from hiring, access to certain types of careers, university acceptance, and others.

This brief history gives context to why many of the same people fighting to change laws that discriminated against women believed abortion was necessary for women to achieve equal rights and equal status. Because men and women experience reproduction so differently, arguments over reproduction began to play a key role in efforts for gender equality. They understood the magnitude of work it would take for women to truly be equal in all aspects of society. We're still working to right some of those injustices today. Even with significant progress, women still face disproportionate setbacks in career, education, and finances due to pregnancy and parenting—setbacks that men typically do not experience in the same way.

At the same time, when individual access to abortion is framed as the primary solution to these inequities, it risks implying that collective and systemic change is not possible.

I want to acknowledge that reproductive decisions are deeply personal and complex, and I'm not suggesting that every woman's decision is driven by inequality. Still, it's important to ask: What kind of society are we building if one of the main ways women can pursue equality is by ending a pregnancy?

Focusing on abortion access alone falls short of the broader transformation needed to ensure that pregnant and parenting women have full and equal access to the same opportunities as their male peers. That deeper work of building supportive systems and communities is still ahead of us.

Despite making great gains in equality between the genders since the 1970s, our society still falls far short from the picture of equality we saw described in 1 Corinthians 11:11-12 and lived out in the ministry of Jesus. This is in part a function of the distorted paradigms about men and women in which we have all been raised. The church, instead of treating men and women with equal dignity and respect, has too often allowed harmful beliefs about gender to take root.

To engage redemptively in the abortion conversation, we must first allow God to reshape how we view and treat one another in the broader pursuit of equality. Rebuilding trust between women and men is essential for honest, healing dialogue about our experiences with reproduction and abortion—experiences that, while different, deeply affect us all.

## NO UTERUS, NO OPINION?

Biologically, a man is just as responsible for creating a pregnancy as a woman, isn't he? And also, biologically, a woman is entirely responsible for nurturing the pregnancy within her body. In a loving relationship between a woman and a man, this biological difference doesn't present a problem. But in a society that too often views unintended pregnancy as solely the woman's responsibility and fails to support her needs, many problems arise. These problems impact women far more dramatically than they do men, physically, financially, practically, and emotionally.

Unintended pregnancy and abortion do affect men, though, in different but sometimes dramatic ways. According to mental health therapist Ginny Lupka,

> When it comes to research on the effects of reproduction on mental health, men's experiences are very under-represented. So when men experience trauma or grief around a pregnancy loss, there is less language and awareness for it, which makes it harder for men to access resources to validate their experiences. Another factor I see in my practice is that women tend to be able to access their grief sooner, while it often takes men a while longer and when it happens it can be intense. One reason is because it's normative in our culture to ask women, "How are you doing?" when they have experienced reproductive loss, while men are rarely asked that question. That disconnect in the way grief is experienced can be very hard on a relationship.[5]

I was working with the leaders of one church to open up prograce conversations for their congregation. They already had women's and men's breakfasts scheduled, meeting separately but around the same time, so they decided to use those venues. At each gathering, they showed a twenty-minute video on the ProGrace approach, then opened it up for discussion. Church leaders were shocked and moved to hear that the number of men who opened up about their lived experience was equal to the number of women. For many of the men, it was their first time sharing about their experience with abortion, and they were compelled to do this only after they heard a reframing of abortion through the lens of grace. Their common theme was, "This is part of my story and I want our congregation to be a safe place for people with similar stories."

To create these safe spaces for dialogue, we must hold the tension of what may seem like conflicting truths. For example, we can acknowledge that the cultural dialogue of "no uterus, no opinion" has emerged from real pain women have experienced when men have been insensitive around reproductive issues. At the same time, achieving the justice and equality we long for will require men to take greater responsibility for pregnancy and parenting. Involving men in conversations about abortion can be difficult, but there are many men who have their own lived experience with abortion, and it's important to validate their emotional experience as well.

Committing to hold space with grace in these tensions is crucial if we hope to foster deeper empathy and connection between women and men.

## WOMEN AND MEN WORKING TOGETHER

Over the years, I have had the privilege of interacting with many men working to make more Christian spaces safe for women. These men in my life have embraced the belief that we are brothers and sisters in Christ. They have humbly considered what it's like to be a woman in our society, and they are moved with compassion to respectfully be part of the solution.

I once asked a man why he so generously supported our pregnancy organization. He got a bit choked up when he said it was because he was a father of three young adult daughters. If any of them ever became pregnant, he would want them to have a safe place for support. He was completely thinking about their welfare, not projecting any possible upheaval or shame he might experience if any of them did face an unintended pregnancy.

Years later, I was facilitating a ProGrace workshop with about fifty people. A man in his late sixties stood up and said he realized during the workshop that he had played the role of a Pharisee in the abortion issue, and he wanted to change. He was part of what his church called their Life Ministry, but he had not understood the reality for women and why they would choose abortion. He realized that—similar to Jesus' description of the Pharisees in Matthew 23:4—he had expected women to carry burdens too heavy for them to bear alone, but he had not been willing to help lift them himself.

He followed through after the workshop and recruited the rest of the ministry team to go through further ProGrace curriculum. As a result, that team wanted to be involved in direct outreach. He discovered that there was a YoungLives group—a group supporting pregnant and parenting teens—that had been meeting at his church but had no previous connection to anyone from the church. He contacted the leader, and she invited his team to a meeting. He sent me a video of his team, all over age forty, joining the games with the young women. He told me that when he heard one of the women tell the story of her pregnancy, he was in awe of her courage and strength.

A different pastor told me one of his church leaders had forced his teenage daughter to have an abortion out of his own shame over the possibility of the pregnancy becoming public. He deeply regretted that he had projected his shame onto her and not listened to what she wanted or needed, so he came to his pastor for guidance. The pastor had discovered the ProGrace language online, and it crystallized his theological understanding in a way that equipped him to counsel his congregant toward grace and healing.

I recently facilitated a breakout session on abortion at a conference for Chicago church leaders. The group was primarily made up of female pastors, ministry leaders, and lay leaders passionate about seeing women valued in their church. The way the few men in the group interacted with the women made an impression on me. They didn't walk out when they saw a room filled mostly with women. They gently and kindly asked the women how they could be involved in a meaningful way in making their church safe for conversations about the abortion issue. They weren't defensive when the women honestly shared that inviting men into the conversation could be complicated and anxiety-inducing. Ultimately, their humility and respect built bridges within that group.

I'm grateful for every man who listens to our podcast, reads our content, donates their time and finances, and participates in our programs. ProGrace recently launched a leaders cohort where there was a spirit of transparency as both men and women shared their connection to the topic of abortion and any places of lived experience. When we equally value the *imago Dei* in every person, this is how God starts to move, bringing women and men together to work for the welfare of all.

I am also grateful for the many women I know who are gracious and Christlike when I know it is challenging for them to have a man as part of this conversation. I'm grateful for women when they courageously say, "That was really hard for me to hear, and this is why," and when they choose to trust men in their community with their views even after experiencing hurt from men in church in the past. I know God is doing a new thing every time I witness a woman share her story in a mixed group or approach her male pastor to open up the conversation in her church for a safe place for others with lived experience.

## Acknowledging Ways Men Have Silenced Women
### —Rev. David Bisgrove

In the ministry year after the Supreme Court overturned *Roe v. Wade*, I led members of our ministry team through the ProGrace curriculum. Working through the topic of abortion in this context would normally lead us to dissect the theology and issue a position paper, but the ProGrace approach is designed instead more for internal reflection than external pronouncements. The curriculum slowed our conversation down by challenging us to deal with the issue as an opportunity for personal spiritual formation and by privileging pastoral concerns over political and theological ones.

The experience reminded me of how my friend and mentor, Tim Keller, would talk about suffering. One can debate suffering on theological, intellectual, and philosophical levels, but what a suffering person needs is compassion, community, and care. The ProGrace approach helped shape our conversations about the relationship between abortion and Christianity in a way that connected us with the real experience of an unintended pregnancy.

There were times in our discussions when we found ourselves slipping into familiar political and scriptural tropes. For example, it isn't uncommon in more conservative theological spaces, like the one our church occupies, to default to defining and defending the child at the expense of reflecting on the experience of the woman carrying the child. It is important to work through how to define the origin of life, but primarily focusing on those kinds of issues can leave the woman undervalued and unheard.

The most transformational part of the experience for me was the space it created for members of our team, made up of both men and women, to share deeply personal and painful experiences of their own. This was a reminder that even though not every theological or social issue requires sensitivity to differences between genders, abortion does. Too many women who regularly attend church don't feel comfortable sharing these kinds of personal stories. Creating an environment that allows for this to happen requires church leaders (and congregants) to be aware of how unhelpful cultural narratives about the differences between men and women can undermine the biblical narrative taught and lived out by Jesus.

For example, the scandals in Christian denominations and organizations reveal that male-dominated structures too often ignore the way women have been exploited and actively silenced in the name of theological authority—authority that is largely exercised by men. In more subtle ways there have been times when I've been part of discussions about women's roles in the church that seem more oriented toward what women can't, shouldn't, and are prohibited from doing than celebrating, encouraging, and supporting what women are and can be doing. Acknowledging the ways the church, and particularly men, might be unjustly silencing or marginalizing women will help foster an environment where both men and women can equally experience the kind of care, compassion, and community necessary in this area.

Reflecting on our experience sitting around the table together and working through the ProGrace curriculum, we were challenged to privilege listening over speaking in ways that we hope will impact how we shepherd and train our congregation. Again, the reason this happened is we individually and collectively wrestled with who Jesus is and what it looks like to follow him in response to this human need. This doesn't discount any conviction to wrestle with the important theological, ethical, and policy-related concerns surrounding abortion. Rather, it helps prioritize our core mission of introducing our neighbors to the compassion and mercy of Jesus—be they inside or outside the church—and to make tangible the way his life-changing and gracious aroma can enter into every part of the human story.

---

*Rev. David Bisgrove served Redeemer Presbyterian Church (RPC) in Manhattan for twenty-five years, the last fifteen as senior pastor of RPC West Side, and is now retired.*

# PART 4

# A Path Forward

# 12

# A United Church

ABOUT FIVE YEARS INTO LEADING the Christian pregnancy organization, I participated in a group with a Chicago pastor who told me one of her congregants was in a leadership position at a pro-choice organization. I hadn't had any success networking with people from that organization, and I begged her to connect us. She finally told me her friend had somewhat reluctantly agreed to meet me and my colleague, but only if her pastor came along. I remember sitting in a lovely restaurant in Chicago's Gold Coast neighborhood, nervously awaiting their arrival.

We shook hands, and then the first words out of this leader's mouth were, "Do you guarantee you are not wearing a wire? And that none of this will be published?" Her fear was genuine, and I later found out she hid her identity to protect her children from protestors who might target them at school and in her neighborhood. I had been taught to be suspicious of people who worked at pro-choice organizations. I was humbled to realize she was suspicious of my intentions because I worked at an organization that had a reputation for aligning with pro-life practices.

I empathized with her fear, and that helped me release some of my own anxiety about talking with her. I asked a lot of questions that day at lunch. She spoke of her theological journey around reproduction and abortion, which had started while she was in medical school. She told me about her passion for neglected children, which is why she and her husband fostered children. And she talked of her passion for women.

She was thoughtful and serious, and I couldn't help but respect her journey. As a result of that conversation, I didn't change my view that abortion was an interruption in God's design for life. However, I began to change my perspective about fellow believers who had different views on abortion. I had to wrestle with the fact that she and I had much more in common regarding the welfare of women and children than we differed on regarding abortion.

Abortion is a complex topic, and we will not fully agree on all aspects of what it means to address it from a Christian perspective. Over the years, I've seen that Christians who are equally committed to following the ways of Jesus can hold different views on how life begins and how we should legislate around that in a pluralistic society. These are important questions for Christians to wrestle with—and we can do so, even in disagreement, with humility and respect.

This kind of posture allows us to unite around shared values, extend grace as we reflect on our past approach to abortion, and work together toward meaningful change.

This is my only hope to bring change and healing in this crucial issue. We can't successfully build bridges in our culture if we don't first unite with our fellow believers. We can commit to shared initiatives that demonstrate our commitment to working together in these areas:

- united in compassion
- united in kingdom priorities
- united in grace

I have seen believers unite around these core areas even while holding points of serious disagreement. If we hold these three areas of common ground up to the two things most Christians are passionate about within the context of abortion—supporting women unconditionally and seeing fewer abortions—we can see that all three areas naturally work together toward the positive outcomes we hope for. Though it may seem counterintuitive to think we will accomplish more by focusing on our inner character and areas of agreement rather than addressing differences or influencing others, this paradox aligns with what Jesus taught about the kingdom of God.

## UNITED IN COMPASSION

As we saw in chapter seven, Jesus shows radical compassion whenever he approaches a human in pain. This kind of *compassion* appears twelve times in the New Testament as a visceral and spiritual response that flows from our inner self, similar to the English expressions, "That breaks my heart," or "I feel sick about that."

Let's look at more occurrences of that word:

> When he saw the crowds, he had compassion on them, because they were harassed and helpless, like sheep without a shepherd. (Matthew 9:36)

> When He came ashore, He saw a large crowd, and felt compassion for them and healed their sick. (Matthew 14:14 NASB)

> Jesus called His disciples to Him, and said, 'I feel compassion for the people, because they have remained with Me now three days and have nothing to eat; and I do not want to send them away hungry, for they might faint on the way.' (Matthew 15:32 NASB)

> Moved with compassion, Jesus touched their eyes; and immediately they regained their sight and followed Him. (Matthew 20:34 NASB)

The word is also used in the following parables, where Jesus is using stories to illustrate how the Godhead relates to people and how we should relate to each other:

> *The unforgiving servant*: And the master of that slave felt compassion, and he released him and forgave him the debt. (Matthew 18:27 NASB)

*The good Samaritan*: But a Samaritan, who was on a journey, came upon him; and when he saw him, he felt compassion. (Luke 10:33 NASB)

*The prodigal son*: So he got up and went to his father. But while he was still a long way off, his father saw him and was filled with compassion for him; he ran to his son, threw his arms around him and kissed him. (Luke 15:20)

Jesus shows us, over and over, that the Father has compassion for us in our human condition. He is consistently moved from the depths of his being to act on our behalf. From the time he thought up the mystery of the incarnation until he allowed his son to be nailed to the cross, the entire story of God revolves around compassion. Being moved to action by compassion and empathy is at the very center of the story of our faith, so it must be at the very center of our response to abortion.

Perhaps one of the harder applications of this call to practice compassion, in the context of our country's abortion debate, is showing compassion to other Christians with whom we disagree.

## UNITED IN KINGDOM PRIORITIES

The partisan divide causes us to think we have nothing in common with the other "side." Most Christians are genuinely trying to hold in balance their concern for both the woman and the child, which can sometimes make them feel like they don't completely fit in either party.

I believe Christ-followers from all denominations and all political persuasions can agree that:

- God creates all life and values all people equally.
- God transforms us through grace.
- Jesus modeled how to care for those in need.

Once we elevate and focus on these, we often begin to discover that we have more in common with fellow believers than we disagree on.

***Our common enemy.*** The political debate supplies us with plenty of enemies to focus on. But this complex issue won't be solved because one political side or another "wins" over the other. "For the weapons of our warfare are not of the flesh, but divinely powerful for the destruction of fortresses" (2 Corinthians 10:4 NASB). The Greek word for "fortresses" in verse 4 is *ochyrōma*, which in this case means "anything on which one relies—of the arguments and reasonings by which a disputant endeavors to fortify his opinion and defend it against his opponent." This sounds a lot like what is happening in the abortion debate, and it's why we need a completely different strategy to communicate truth. Why would we ever want to fight with the weapons of the world, which harm us all in the end, when we can partner with God, whose ways are anchored in deep love for all of humanity?

We read in Ephesians, "We aren't fighting against human enemies but against rulers, authorities, forces of cosmic darkness, and spiritual powers of evil in the heavens. Therefore, pick up the full armor of God so that you can stand your ground on the evil day and after you have done everything possible to still stand" (Ephesians 6:12-13 CEB). The enemy in the abortion debate is not humans. It's not people on the opposing political side or with different moral convictions. It's not lawmakers, protestors, or policy advocates. It's not people with lived experience of unintended pregnancy or abortion. The enemies are the rulers and forces of evil that place disproportionate responsibility on women, create scarcity of resources, focus on individual responsibility to the exclusion of collective responsibility, and tolerate abuses of power.

***Our common part in the problem.*** Part of becoming prograce means taking the time to look at how we may have unintentionally absorbed these narratives and, as a result, become part of the problem, since Jesus says all vile actions "come from inside" (Mark 7:23). If we continue to think all the problems in the abortion debate originate outside of ourselves and we simply blame the other side, we will

never see transformation. Those are the weapons the world continues
to use. Aren't we tired of them?

Similar to Jesus' command that we should look at the log in our
own eye first, Paul says, "What business is it of mine to judge those
outside the church? Are you not to judge those inside? God will judge
those outside" (1 Corinthians 5:12-13). It's time for us to repent from
blaming outside forces and lift our eyes to how Jesus demonstrates
the kingdom of God in action.

Once we do this, we can find our way to look inward first, evaluating our values with kingdom values, which allows us to find
common ground with other believers.

***Our common ground and shared values.*** I still believe what I tried
(unsuccessfully) to convey at my high school reunion: Providing
unconditional support for women and desiring to see fewer abortions don't need to be mutually exclusive.

First, offering unconditional support for women does not increase
the number of abortions. We may have absorbed this idea from existing narratives, but the data doesn't support it. In fact, statistics
indicate the opposite is likely true. When two out of three women
cite multiple factors influencing their decision to have an abortion—
such as financial constraints, care for other children, and partner-
related reasons[1]—we can hypothesize that if these needs were ad-
dressed, more women might continue their pregnancies.

Second, one can desire a reduction in the number of abortions
while also offering women unconditional support that is free of persuasion or hidden agendas. Wanting something and manipulating
someone to achieve it are two entirely different things. While I have
witnessed individuals using pressure tactics to try to decrease
abortion, I have encountered many more who choose a different way:
They listen to understand, empathize with emotional realities, and
refrain from giving advice—entrusting it all to God.

The values themselves are not the issue. The problem lies in how we
pursue these values—this is where we can make most of our mistakes.

For example, if we value seeing fewer abortions, we must ensure that our approach never unintentionally devalues women, diminishes their dignity, minimizes their experiences, or overlooks the complex realities they face. Likewise, if we value providing unconditional support to women, we must ensure that our approach doesn't present access to abortion as the only form of support. That too can unintentionally devalue, diminish, minimize, and overlook women and their experiences.

True support means addressing the economic, relational, and cultural pressures that can make continuing a pregnancy feel impossible. And by God's design, when we offer this kind of support to pregnant women, we also honor the dignity of their children. This is why these two values do not have to be in conflict with each other. In fact, both can be upheld by Christians whose primary aim is to respond to the issue of abortion in a Jesus-centered way rather than simply aligning with a partisan perspective.

One way to stay grounded as we seek to build bridges with fellow believers is to expand our understanding of the complexity surrounding abortion. The political debate often demands that we choose between two moral concerns—support for women or reducing the number of abortions. But as Christians, we know there are many more ethical concerns at play. These include:

- Cultural narratives that minimize the dignity and worth of people made in the image of God
- Unmet emotional, social, and financial needs that drive many abortions
- False assumptions we have developed about who seeks abortions and why
- Systemic norms that place the burden of pregnancy and parenting on individuals, and particularly women
- Gender inequality in our society—and more grievously, within the church

Addressing these concerns reflects God's care and compassion far more than our national debate, and they are conversations every Christian can engage in as part of our ongoing work to build the kingdom of God. Seeking to understand and find solutions to these deeper issues offers a uniquely Christian response to abortion—one that is compelling and hope-giving.

## UNITED IN GRACE

When we talk about approaching the abortion conversation with grace, the first thing that may come to mind is demonstrating grace to people with lived experience of unintended pregnancy and abortion. This is natural, since much of the judgment and shame in this conversation has historically been directed toward them. However, when we broaden our perspective beyond a narrow focus on individuals making this decision and begin to include our corporate responsibility, extending grace takes on an expansive meaning that is crucial to Christian unity. Personally, I have struggled to extend grace to other believers I perceive as causing harm to women facing abortion decisions. In my frustration, it has been easy to jump to conclusions and make judgments about these fellow believers.

But I have become convinced that grace is essential for productive conversations with other believers about abortion. No matter who I'm talking to, I've found the first way I can extend grace is by asking questions and listening to understand. This rule of thumb is very helpful when anger floods my brain and I otherwise cannot find gracious words to say. Once I have listened enough to access my own empathy for the person speaking, I try to respond by first highlighting something they said that I agree with. I do approach areas of disagreement in conversations, but I attempt to only do so with people I already have established trust with and who I am intentionally building community with. I have never found it productive to try and solve areas of disagreement with someone I haven't first established common ground with, enough so that we will give each other the benefit of the doubt as we work through challenging topics.

When we approach conversations with grace instead of judgment, we find that most of us can agree on the essence of what we want for our church and our community, whether or not we consider ourselves politically pro-life or pro-choice. Once we know we are aligned theologically *more* than we disagree politically, we can then work together to transform our churches and communities into spaces that transcend the political divide to reflect the heart of God. And that is the type of community we need to be if we are ever to see all of the positive outcomes both sides long to see. It may feel counterintuitive, but those outcomes only become possible when we take our eyes off other people's behavior, which we can't control, and put them onto our own behavior, which we can.

Even if we don't understand every talking point of a political side, we can believe that most Christians have chosen their political position because, at least on some level, it seems to them the most Christlike option. Once we understand this, once we get into the habit of intentionally believing the best about our brothers and sisters in Christ, we are more empowered to find ways to work for both the woman and the child. This will not allow us to escape the very real tension of this complex issue, but it will at the very least demonstrate that God loves, values, and advocates for each person far more than either political party can, and this is a much-needed message of hope for our present time.

Seeking unity is *not* asking pro-life Christians to value the child any less; it's an opportunity to value the child *more*, as our collective efforts will do far more to promote their welfare than our division will.

Seeking unity also is *not* asking pro-choice Christians to value the woman any less; it's an opportunity to value the woman *more*, as we collaborate to have different conversations that elevate the voices of women in Christian spaces and ultimately make our communities safe to approach.

Unity helps us prioritize the goal of becoming more like Jesus. Unity paves the way for more Christians to enter the conversation without fear of partisan conflict. It frees up our mental energy and time to do the work of becoming more approachable and welcoming. Unity will lead to *more* commitment from Christians to work for the dignity and welfare of both women and children, not less.

## Unity Begins with Our Posture
### —Andrew Hanauer

I travel around the country as part of my job, and many times when I take an Uber the driver asks, "What do you do for work?"

I say, "I'm trying to make the country less divided."

They usually laugh first and say something like, "Good luck with that." Then they tell me how excited they are that our organization exists because almost nobody likes our country's division.

But the most interesting part is they say something like, "Well, let me tell you why we're divided." And invariably, it's the fault of everyone they don't like. It's the Democrats' fault, or it's the Republicans' fault, or mass media, or whatever. We're ready to look everywhere for the problem except the mirror.

We have to start by asking, *Who am I? What am I doing? What am I putting out into the world?* Because you can't control what other people do. You can't control what politicians do, but you can control how you influence people around you.

The division we have in our country today is a spiritual crisis. It's about more than just *what kind of country we are going to be;* it's also about *what kind of person I am going to be.*

At our core as human beings, we are wired to want to belong. We want to be in a group. A group gives us protection. It gives us a sense of stability. It gives us meaning. It gives us a way to understand the rules of life and of living. Human beings are going to search for belonging. And if they're not finding it in a healthy religious community or in a local community of some kind, they will look for it online. They're going to look for it wherever they can find it. And one of the easiest ways to find it is to ask, *Who hates the same people I hate?*

We have become people who are looking for their belonging and their identity in politics. Politics can excite us. You go to a rally, you hear an inspirational candidate, and maybe you believe that it's really, really important who wins and who loses. But at the end of the day, politics will not fill the spiritual holes in our lives. It won't give us a vision for human flourishing and understanding the nature of the universe and our purpose on earth. And so it's an incomplete identity in that way.

Of course, we're also finding out that politics is also really negative in many ways. It pits us against each other. It convinces us that we're right all the time. It tells us that our neighbors are actually our enemies. Our faith, on the other hand, tells us that even if our neighbors are our enemies, we're still supposed to love them.

If faith communities are healthy, they give you all those aspects of belonging, a language, and a set of values that teach us how to be in the world with others who disagree with us. Many faith communities all across the country are already doing this, but they're up against loud, angry, divisive rhetoric that is often much better funded.

So a lot of this has to come down to *Is my church healthy? Am I healthy?*

When it comes to abortion or other disagreements over policy, the question is not how to shift your beliefs or anything like that, but more, how do you be the best version of someone who holds those beliefs? How do you best understand perspectives that aren't yours? It's not about tamping down your beliefs; it's about showing up in a way that compels anyone else to want to know what you believe in. The *way* you engage is how you build trust and get anyone to care what you say.

In a challenging conversation with someone you disagree with, it's ideal if you mutually disarm. It's ideal if you have a setting where both people participate that way. However, something that I see as foundational to what Jesus taught us is that we, as Christians, should disarm first. If the other person's not going to disarm, I should still disarm, and I should be able to go to that person to admit my own doubts first because it's a model for how we can all be. And maybe the other person won't reciprocate, but I can't control that. I can control myself.

We support faith communities and leaders to be the opposite of our divided, disconnected culture, to come together across divides, and to be a model for our country.

---

*Andrew Hanauer is the founder and CEO of One America Movement, a multi-faith nonprofit organization that supports the American faith community in reducing toxic division.*

# 13

# Conversations That Create Community

So much of my personal journey to becoming prograce has been guided by conversations that expanded my understanding, deepened my empathy, and as a result, transformed me. These have been conversations with people from both political affiliations, pastors, women's health care professionals, Bible scholars, church members, as well as people who have the lived experience of unintended pregnancy and abortion.

And yet, the question I seem to get most from Christians is how to have conversations with a woman in that short moment of time when she's considering abortion, as if those conversations are the key to making a difference. I don't give exhaustive instructions for conversations with women considering abortion, because we are speaking to women all the time. Every time we express judgment for someone facing an unintended pregnancy or choosing to have an abortion, we're telling women what they can expect from us. When we've already spoken words of fear and shame into a reality that they are now experiencing, they most likely will not bother coming to us for support. Who would?

Instead, I focus on having better, grace-centered conversations about abortion with *each other* in ways that transform our hearts and transcend political divides. We set the culture every time we speak, no matter who we're speaking to.

We can't represent something we haven't first become, and becoming prograce—having our minds and hearts transformed through empathy and grace—is a process that will be guided by the

Holy Spirit. There are no talking points we can memorize that will be
more effective than simply leaning into God's invitation to see people
as he does in our day-to-day life. This is the bedrock for having conversations that build community.

## LISTEN FIRST

Even if we are bursting with new thoughts and insights, we are more
likely to have conversations that build community if we come in committed to listening first. I have really struggled with this in my own
life. Early on, I would feel stuck in thoughts such as: *Isn't my most
important responsibility to state my moral and political views on
abortion? If I listen to others with differing experiences or views, will I
lose my own convictions?* I remember facing near-panic in some conversations because of these thoughts. The best help I found was to
listen intentionally to the Holy Spirit during every conversation.

   ***Listen to the Holy Spirit.*** Sometimes, I was so nervous in conversations that all I could do was silently pray, "Spirit of truth, reveal
truth" (John 16:13). In response, the Holy Spirit often directed my
thoughts back to the example of Jesus. I'm amazed by how well Jesus
saw each person he interacted with. He was observant. He listened
to people, and he listened to what his father was doing (John 5:19).
He listened so well that when he did speak, it was the exact message
that person needed to hear to move closer to God.

   When practicing listening to the Holy Spirit, one way I try to
discern whether or not it really is the Spirit I'm sensing is to evaluate
if what I'm hearing lines up with God's character as revealed in Jesus,
because Jesus said the Spirit will always "glorify me because it is
from me that he will receive what he will make known to you"
(John 16:14). We can trust that God, who knows and loves the person
we're talking to, will guide us. With God and with people, there is
always more to understand, experience, and grow into, so maintaining this posture of listening is a lifelong practice as we learn how
to navigate this conversation.

*Listen to lived experiences.* Listening is one of the best ways we can demonstrate to people that we value them and validate their experience. When we start applying grace to the abortion conversation, chances are high that one of the first people we listen to when discussing abortion will be someone who has experienced unintended pregnancy or abortion, since 1 in 4 women will have an abortion in their lifetime, and around 40 percent of all pregnancies are unintended.[1] Partners and family often share in these experiences as well.

Over the years, in conversation and after speaking events, I've had the privilege of interacting with dozens of women—and men—who tell me about their past lived experience. One of my colleagues from the pregnancy organization once spoke at a church, outlining how we need a new mindset and language to be a safe community. After her presentation, the pastor's wife leaned over to my colleague and said, "No one in this church knows this, but this is our story."

People are carrying their stories and not talking about them—including pastors and church leaders. There are most likely many people in our churches who have already experienced an abortion and don't feel they can discuss it with anyone in their community, whether it happened five months, five years, or fifty years ago.

If someone confides in you about their lived experience, it is a great honor, because it means they perceive you as safe to be vulnerable with. When this happens to me, I first thank the person for trusting me with their story. I tell them I'm here to listen if they want to share more, but I have no expectations. I let them direct the conversation.

I don't want to dig deeper than the person wants to go, so often I'll say something general like, "Is there anything else you would like to tell me about your experience?" From there, I follow their lead. People have a wide range of feelings about their experience, and I learned early on to not assume what that is.

I don't ask a woman why she made the decision she did; I'm listening in order to understand whatever she chooses to share. I want her to know that I see her, that I understand there was a lot more going on than her simply making a decision, and that I don't view her any differently than I did before this conversation. I also don't assume she needs to process the decision any further. If she does express a desire to process her decision, I have trusted nonprofit partners I can connect her with (visit prograce.org to see our list of partners). I also know that mental health professionals can provide helpful counsel if someone needs to process the emotional complexity of reproductive loss. Very importantly, I make sure to keep everything I'm told confidential unless someone specifically gives me permission to share with others.

More and more Christians with the lived experience of abortion or unintended pregnancy are joining the ProGrace community, and they have played a crucial role in leading the change to make Christian spaces safe for others with similar experiences. I'm so grateful they trust their fellow believers with their stories, and I believe God will use them in powerful ways.

***Listen to understand.*** Most of us can't help reacting a bit to a statement from someone who holds a different political view than we do. We are conditioned to feel morally superior to others through social media algorithms and news pundits. This means we need to actively work toward listening to understand people who are different from us in order to shed our own bias. By listening to understand, rather than listening to respond, we make room for transformation in ourselves and also in the person we're talking with.

Even knowing this, I am often tempted to give others advice instead of asking questions. So I have an arsenal of questions ready to start the conversation with other believers.

Questions for conversations with our family or close friends:

- What is your perception of the Christian response to abortion?
- How does that compare with what you've experienced in our family?

- What would you like to see Christians do more or less of?
- How do you think we could engage more like Jesus?

Questions for conversations with people in our church:

- What do you think our church communicates in the way we address abortion?
- Do you think this is a safe place for you personally to have conversations about unintended pregnancy and abortion? Why or why not?
- What could we do to pave the way for more honest conversation?
- How do you feel our church's response to abortion lines up with our commitment to follow Jesus? Are they in line with each other? Or does something feel off? And if so, what?

It's okay, and actually quite healthy, if our first conversations consist only of us listening. People can tell if we enter a conversation with compassion and a desire to listen to understand. It lays the foundation for trust. Once we lead with questions and listen to understand, we will build trust. And once trust is in place, we will have an opportunity to speak, even if not in that particular conversation.

## LANGUAGE CHANGES

People often tell me that when they are talking about abortion, they have their intentions and thoughts straight in their heads, but as soon as they open their mouths, their words become jumbled and their anxiety rises that they will say the wrong thing. This is why people ask me all the time for conversation tools and templates.

The most essential part of our speaking isn't our tools or our script, but that we've already listened well—to God, to our own story, and to the stories of others. It is helpful to be aware of the defensiveness that might come up in us, because a critical piece of productive conversation is giving people permission to stop us if we say something they don't understand or feel upset about.

These tools are suggestions based on my experience engaging in conversations with people from both sides in this debate. Even as we use them, the most important thing is to check in for understanding and ensure we don't begin a one-sided conversation.

*Lead with theology.* It's most productive to start conversations with other Christians with theological points Christians from all denominations agree on.

- Prioritizing becoming more like Jesus in our response to abortion
- Aligning with God's equal value, dignity, and worth for every person
- Relying on the transformative power of grace to bring change
- Looking inward and evaluating our response rather than trying to change others

We might want to stop after this to see how the person we're talking to is responding. Even if the conversation moves to discuss our different political leanings, I always try to stay anchored in this theological framework.

*Word substitutions.* Certain words can unintentionally trigger defenses and shut down a conversation in a moment. Often this can cloud our thinking, making it seem like we disagree when we really agree, so it's best to avoid or change the words and phrases we use. These words and phrases have developed culturally, not based on any messages from Scripture. Our willingness to let them go is one way we can live out the words of Paul: "I have become all things to all people so that by all possible means I might save some. I do all this for the sake of the gospel, that I may share in its blessings" (1 Corinthians 9:22-23).

These are simple language changes we can make for ourselves. Other people may or may not notice, and that's okay. Our goal isn't to change their language, but to be confident that we are being more clear about what we want to communicate. The following are some examples of word substitutions I use.

Remove: *mothers*

Replace: *women*

Referring to pregnant women as mothers can communicate that we are primarily interested in helping them if they continue the pregnancy, or we only recognize their identity in relation to their child. We want to convey that we care about women in all that they are, including, but not limited to, as a mother.

Remove: *unborn child or fetus*

Replace: *child*

Even though both *unborn child* and *fetus* are medically accurate terms, each is associated with one political side. Furthermore, using *unborn child* perpetuates the wrong stereotype, that we only care about birth and don't do much afterward. Using *fetus* perpetuates the wrong stereotype that we are trying to downplay anything that happens with a child before birth. Using *child* is the best way I've found to communicate that I'm committed to supporting both the woman and child equally during and after pregnancy.

Remove: *choose life, decision for life*

Replace: *carry to term, have the child*

*Decision for life* perpetuates an inaccurate stereotype that abortion is a determined decision against life, rather than a response to complex sociological and personal factors that make continuing a pregnancy seem impossible.

Remove: *post-abortive woman (or man)*

Replace: *people who have had an abortion,* or *people with lived experience of abortion*

*Post-abortive* is a term that confers identity, as if having an abortion is a threshold someone crosses, and they are a different person afterward. It's worth pondering why this is a term commonly used in the abortion context, but not others. We don't see any precedence in Scripture for a Christ-follower taking on an identity other than a child of God (1 John 3:1), one who is loved by God (Romans 1:7), or the righteousness of God in Christ (2 Corinthians 5:21).

Remove: *out of wedlock*

Replace: *parents not married* or *single parent*

We can wonder why the thirteenth-century word *wedlock* has not been used to describe marriage for longer than any of us know, but it is still paired with "out of" to describe children being born to parents not married. What we do know is this phrase has always carried stigma, and that most likely explains its staying power. It's time to let it go.

To consider: *pro-life* and *pro-choice*

It's only clear what the terms *pro-life* and *pro-choice* mean when they are used to describe a political position. Any use or definition beyond that gets murky, so it's best to limit them to that context. It's also worth evaluating when and where we want to use the words to describe our political conviction, since the words are attached to harmful stereotypes and cause deep division. Having conversations without these labels creates a much safer environment for people to open up about their own thoughts and experiences.

## LEAD WITH LIKENESS

In order to build unity in the church, it is essential we look for places of agreement—of which there are many—and lead our conversations by naming them. There is certainly a place for discussing disagreement on complicated questions with other believers, but those conversations are only edifying when grounded in trust. In this case, trust means an understanding that we assume the best in each other and will move quicker to empathy than to judgment. When we intentionally spend time talking about points of agreement with other Christians—or any humans, for that matter—we are building crucial trust that can support more difficult conversations to come.

After we've found common ground in our theology, here are some further topics we can bring up with other Christians to find points of unity.

- How can we become more like Jesus in the way we think and talk about abortion?

- In your opinion, what would it take to make Christian spaces safe for honest conversations about this issue?

- Do you ever feel conflicted about the abortion issue? If so, in what ways?

- If we made more room for nuance in this conversation, what questions would you want to ask other believers?

- How can we create a culture of grace in our families and churches?

- What would it look like to make Christian spaces safer for people with lived experience of abortion?

I didn't feel ready for many of the conversations I had around abortion. I was concerned a colleague or board members would misunderstand my intentions. I was afraid a neighbor would think I didn't see the needs of women. I got tense answering questions from donors who wanted to know how we were preventing abortions. To this day, there are still times I have to remind myself to stop, ask questions, and listen.

## STOP, ASK, LISTEN

My son Noah recently asked me if I thought this book would make any difference in how Christians respond to the issue of abortion. He is currently a senior in high school and has many of the same concerns about Christians as in the studies referenced in previous chapters. I started preaching to him about how good God is, because it's something I really want him to know, even when people who profess to follow him don't represent that goodness. Then the ever-faithful Holy Spirit nudged me to stop talking and instead ask a question. So I did.

I asked Noah what he meant by his question, and if he could please tell me more. He told me he didn't see good things Christians were doing or had done in the world. He told me the vocal Christian response he sees on social media is angry and condemning. He talked about the crusades and the way the church justified slavery and colluded with the Nazis.

I had a million things I wanted to share with him—like how many of the Christians I interact with really do reflect Jesus, or the way Christians nursed plague victims when no one else would, fought to end slavery, and hid Jewish people from the Nazis. But I didn't, because this wasn't the time or place to tell him all the wonderful things Christians have done. It was time to listen to his disillusionment about the equally valid, terrible things that have been done in the name of Christ, to be genuinely sorry for those things.

By prompting me to ask questions and listen, God gently reminded me that he never asks me to take responsibility for the outcomes in someone else's life. Instead, he calls me to be inwardly transformed in ways that naturally reflect his character. That includes caring enough to listen deeply and seek genuine understanding—just as Jesus did. If I'm trying to reflect him, then becoming more like him must remain my primary goal.

## Retraining Our Minds to Build Bridges
### —Christy Vines

The work of the Center for Peacebuilding and Conflict Transformation at Fuller Theological Seminary foregrounds peacebuilding as a core competency for Christian ministry and cultivates transformative Christian leadership rooted in compassion, spiritual formation, and restorative justice, equipping individuals to serve as agents of healing in a fractured world. Grounded in practices of peacebuilding, reconciliation, and community engagement, the Center integrates theological depth with real-world impact. Our work is focused on discovering how to bring people together across divides, lessening the defensive postures that our brains are wired to push us toward.

When we know that we are going into a conversation with someone who has a very different opinion or perspective than us, our brains immediately switch into defense mode. So if we come into a challenging conversation thinking "My job is to debate this," our brains immediately start to look at the other person as the enemy. We immediately start to focus on what makes us different from one another. There is no way to go from that starting position to a positive, healthy outcome.

When we seek common ground, our brain starts to seek things that make us alike, and our defensiveness goes down. We observe this in physical cues, where people's shoulders drop, they breathe sighs of relief, and they even smile. If we enter into our conversations thinking, "I don't care how long it takes me. I'm going to find something we have in common," our brains are primed to see something positive rather than negative.

Then the next step is deep listening—listening without the idea or responsibility of defense or debate. This is something most of us don't learn, especially in Western civilization and in particular in the United States. We are taught from birth to communicate in order to influence, to inform, and to win, so that is our style of communication. From the moment we speak our first word or scream and cry, our brain starts recognizing that when we talk, we have an impact. We get people to move.

When we reverse that survival instinct, our brain actually changes its job. Instead of being wired to defend and debate, which closes it off to any information that doesn't support that goal, a filter goes down and our brain becomes curious. Our brain seeks more information to learn and to lessen the distance between the two individuals. So everything, then, is in service of learning and listening.

I often point Christians to Paul, who I believe was biblically one of the most empathically intelligent individuals, at least as we see him shared in the New Testament. There's a point when he's addressing the Greeks, and rather than destroy and tear down their cultural norms, he essentially says, "I've listened and

I've learned, and I understand who you are," he tells them in Acts 17:22-23 (MSG), "It is plain to see that you take your religion seriously. When I arrived here the other day, I was fascinated with all the shrines I came across. And then I found one inscribed, TO THE GOD NOBODY KNOWS. I'm here to introduce you to this God so you can worship intelligently, know who you're dealing with." He's telling them Jesus can be implanted right in the center of their beliefs, and he's introducing them to Jesus in a context that makes sense for them. One of the worst things we can do as Christians is debate and defend the Gospel without being curious about who it is we're actually sharing Jesus with. Throughout the gospels, when Jesus engages with somebody he doesn't know, he asks them questions. Then he shares himself in a way that is relevant.

One thing that can really help change how we engage on divisive topics is to remember that if you cannot say "I understand why this person holds the position they hold," then it's your job to keep asking questions and listening. Out of that, I would be hard-pressed to find too many people who won't find some point of connection that allows the defensive posture to soften and allows them to see the other person as the full expression of their history, of everything that has brought them to that point. It's magical what happens as a result.

---

*Christy Vines is the executive director of the Center for Peacebuilding and Conflict Transformation at Fuller Theological Seminary, a center for theological reflection, research, and training in biblically grounded, trauma-informed peacebuilding. Christy is also the founder and former president of Ideos Institute.*

# 14

# Being ProGrace: A Picture

ABOUT FIVE YEARS INTO LEADING the pregnancy organization, I had confidence that our programs were meeting the needs of women in a way that communicated dignity and value. We had a team of professional counselors who listened to women, helped them see their strengths, and designed a case management plan to widen their support system. Our staff and volunteers who interacted with women outside these counseling sessions were also trained in question-asking models. We had transitioned from two websites to one, and that website was transparent about our practices, our mission, and our faith.

I was encouraged to hear the survey responses and continued research where women described the impact of our programs. At the same time, I was keenly aware that many of our clients and their children had more needs. We were a small organization with a focus and specialty on the experience of unintended pregnancy, so we couldn't create programs to meet every practical and emotional need.

We decided to put our energy into developing therapeutic support groups for women during their pregnancy and up to one year after. We hypothesized that if we could continue to provide the emotional support that would reinforce a sense of identity and belonging, women could move forward in a much stronger place, impacting their future and the future of their child if they were parenting. The research began to show that through these groups, a woman's support system shifted from her counselor to the other members, starting the process of building an ongoing supportive community.

However, we only had the resources to serve women this way for one year, and we knew they would have longer-term needs than we could meet. Our team was already starting to dream about churches being this kind of safe and supportive community, and we had volunteers who shared that vision. So we tried several pilot programs to connect volunteers from our partner churches with the women we served in our on-site support groups.

I was so sure this would work, and I felt deflated when my team reported to me the reasons each of these pilots weren't working. The church volunteers felt uncomfortable and ill-equipped when they tried to connect with our clients over dinner in a group setting. Or they didn't know how to build a relationship one-on-one when it felt so forced. Our clients said, "Why would I want to connect with someone from a church? Religion just makes me feel worse about myself."

I remember sitting in a conference room as they were describing the failure of the most recent pilot, and I finally asked if we could stop and pray. All I could think to pray was, "God, from everything we know about you and what you set up your church to be, we believe it's your will that the women we serve would have the opportunity to be connected with people from a church. Show us what to do."

## A SAFE COMMUNITY

Several months later, my team came back and told me a story. A young woman in one of our support groups was coming to the end of her time with us but didn't want her group to end, so she approached her church. She told them she was grateful they had initially referred her to our organization, but now she needed more. She saw no place for her at the church since she didn't fit in the college group because she was a mom, and they didn't have any programs or groups for single moms. She asked if she could start a similar support group at the church, and they said yes.

She did all this on her own. This wasn't us guessing what she wanted or what would meet her needs—it was her initiative, leadership, and self-care. This also wasn't us trying to connect women who weren't familiar with the church to strangers at churches they had never heard of. This was a Christian woman going to her own church and asking them to create a space for her to belong in this season of life she was in.

One of our counselors attended that church and volunteered to help facilitate the group on her own time because we didn't have the resources to staff it. The group quickly doubled in size as the women involved told their friends. Some women from the group started a cleaning business together. One woman said she had never considered going to college because she had a child, until she watched someone else in the group return to school. Another woman told us she came to the first group thinking she would never attend the worship service, but a group of them went one Sunday, and she joined them. She loved it so much she brought her boyfriend.

In short, the women were thriving, and I was ecstatic. I wondered if the church's leaders realized that through this group, they were being the hands and feet of Jesus in a way that could revolutionize the abortion debate. I thought of all the other churches who longed to be the hands and feet of Jesus in this way as well. These questions were seeds for a vision I would later pursue full-force to help churches and congregants, not just pregnancy organization staff, embody the ProGrace approach. When my colleague and I sat around my dining room table and wrote the first piece of what is now the ProGrace curriculum, we wondered if anyone would be interested. We then tested the curriculum through an in-person workshop with seven Chicago churches who responded so positively to the content that, in August 2016, we launched ProGrace as an organization to equip Christians nationwide who were ready for a new way to think and talk about abortion. So much has changed in our country since then, and I sometimes look back in amazement, thinking about all the things I never saw coming. Pastors have become less willing to talk about abortion as a result of the deepening political divide. The global pandemic threatened to shut down churches and moved so much programming online instead of in community. Then, much to my surprise, *Roe v. Wade* was overturned in 2022, prompting people on both sides of the debate to rethink their beliefs amid a changing legal landscape.

And yet, my vision remains the same. I still remember the names of the women in that first support group. I can hear them telling their stories, seeing footage of their baptisms, hearing the hope in their voices. I'm still convinced that as we are transformed, God will help us transform our Christian spaces—direct service organizations and churches like I've already seen, but also families, small groups, schools, universities, and ministries. I'm still praying the same prayer, "Lord, we know it's your will that people with this lived experience would find belonging, connection, and support in faith communities. Show us what to do."

## GOD IS AT WORK IN THE CHURCH

The church that first hosted an on-site support group for pregnant women from our pregnancy organization was Willow Creek—one of the largest churches in Chicago, led by a pastor who, unbeknownst to us, was harming women within the church for the entire timespan of our group there.

I still feel the tension about the abuse of power happening behind the scenes at Willow Creek and the beautiful, transformative work we saw God do in that group. The church's leadership team said yes to hosting the support group because of a genuine commitment to be welcoming and to show love in all they do. If they hadn't said yes, I don't know where ProGrace would be today. Seeing pregnant women welcomed into their church family gave me confidence that we could see it in churches throughout the country. I've had to walk through feelings of confusion, anger, and discouragement after learning that this all happened at a time when this church was in the midst of clergy abuse. And yet, I believe that God was present and the women in the group experienced true community.

Our challenge is to keep looking for the places God is at work, even when they dramatically defy our expectations; to stay alert to the good work of God happening in the church, even when we feel angry or disillusioned because of the harm we've seen inflicted by Christians. The thing is, we are the church. We aren't separate from everything that is happening—we are all part of an interdependent body, which God has promised to fill, empower, and lead. I don't want to give up on the church, because I don't want to give up on his promise.

## WHAT WILL IT TAKE?

Thousands of people have now used the ProGrace approach and have built stronger relationships with their families, friends, and community members in the process. I can't count the number of times someone has told me they told a friend or family member they were participating in a ProGrace course, and as they described the approach, the person listening said, "I've never told you this, but I experienced abortion."

Undoing decades, centuries, potentially millennia of distorted thinking about abortion is lifelong spiritual work. It's our most important work, because all our actions flow from this internal place. Doing this work means we're going to pass on a different legacy to our kids, one that prioritizes being like Jesus over all else. There is no way to measure the ongoing, generational impact it can have within a Christian family, church, and community when we speak with a focus on human dignity and grace. That's why becoming prograce is not about following a how-to manual for forming a Christian response to abortion; it is ultimately about spiritual formation.

I dream of an institutional ecosystem that supports women—an ecosystem that includes local churches, pregnancy organizations, single-parent ministries, universities, and health centers—but the only way our institutions will change is if we let God begin his trans-formative work in us first. The US culture is programmed for quick results, quick change, often leading us to think we can bypass people. But the deep work of the Holy Spirit is profoundly personal and usually takes much, much longer than any of us would like.

I'm not sure what the abortion conversation or even the church will look like in the next ten or twenty years. We are living in times of major upheaval—some of it necessary, some of it tragic, and all of it bringing significant uncertainty into our lives. But now and forever, our faith affirms that the church of Jesus Christ will endure and will be a force of love in our communities.

## Holding Abortion Stories with Grace
### —Stacey and David

**Stacey:** For fifteen years, I carried the weight of my abortion in silence. No one knew about my abortion except for my husband, who was there with me. We planned on taking our abortion story to the grave. And for a long time, that worked—until it didn't.

A few years ago, we were working with a church that was very involved in the pro-life movement, and the things I observed, the conversations I heard, the certainty with which people spoke—it all triggered emotions I had long buried.

In the middle of the night one night, I woke my husband up and asked, "What would you think about me talking to David about our abortion?" I was secretly hoping he would say no, because if he wasn't on board, I wouldn't do it; it was our story together. But he said yes. I had always known that David (our friend and ministry partner) would be safe to talk to about our abortion, I just never thought I would actually need to do it.

Early the next morning, before I could change my mind, I sent David a text message and told him, "There's a part of my story that no one knows about and I think we should have this conver-sation." A few days later, we sat down to have that conversation, and I was terrified. What if he saw me differently? What if he confirmed my worst fear—that if people knew this part of my story, they wouldn't see me as worthy of love or grace, and they would ultimately walk away?

***David:*** As a pastor over the years, when someone wants to come and talk, I usually assume it's about something I did or something that they want to be different. So when Stacey asked me to talk, I came in thinking, "Okay, I've known Stacey long enough to know that no matter what she comes with, we love each other and we're family." Then she started talking about her own heart and life, and I had to shift modes. I thought, "Oh, this is not anything to do with me. I just need to be here, like really *be here*."

***Stacey:*** I told him, "I need you to understand all of my backstory before I tell you this part of my story. Here's how it was growing up in my home, and here's the harmful things that I heard and that I experienced, and all the reasons that led us to making the decision that we did." I remember getting to a certain point and I couldn't even look up because there was so much shame, and so much uncertainty about what would happen now that someone knew the part of my story that had been buried for so long. But that conversation, and the grace I encountered, changed everything.

***David:*** I pretty much just listened for twelve minutes or so while she spoke. And then when she was done, one of the first questions I asked her was, "How do you feel now?"

***Stacey:*** I had never been asked that question before. From my experience with pro-life Christians, there was so much value put on the life of the child that I began to believe my life no longer had value. So for someone to ask me how I felt after hearing my abortion story was huge for me.

For people who have this lived experience, you often feel like you don't deserve to grieve the loss of your child or the loss of what you expected your future to look like, and that hinders a lot of women and men from finding true healing because you don't feel like you're worth it. So when someone asks, *How are you feeling with all of this?* it gives you space to process the emotions that ultimately you need to process in order to truly heal.

**David:** I knew she was telling me about this experience for the sake of her own heart, because it was something she needed to do, and my respect for her only increased. She was moving toward a place of greater flourishing in life, and I knew it would not only benefit her, but that God would love other people through this redemption.

**Stacey:** Shortly after my conversation with David, I happened upon ProGrace through a podcast. And it was the first time I had heard and experienced Christians having a conversation around abortion that wasn't harmful to women with this lived experience. It was the first time I heard a group of Christians holding the life of the woman as equally valuable and precious as the life of the child.

I decided to join a cohort for people interested in starting a ProGrace conversation at their church and invited David to join me. It meant the world to me to have my friend and pastor join me in the cohort, not just saying that he supported me and my journey to healing, but showing me through his actions that he was in my corner.

**David:** There's a huge ripple effect to what Stacey is doing, giving people permission to be healed in so many other areas of their lives. If we as a church are a safe place for talking about abortion, then a lot of other things can come up too. That whole shame piece is gone.

**Stacey:** We have recently started working with a new church, and I talked with the leadership team there about starting a small group for women who have lived experience with abortion. They were 100 percent in from day one. I was intentional about creating a confidential, safe space for these women. Very few people know when or where we're meeting, and it has already been so, so good. One woman has already shared that it's been almost fifty years since she had her abortion, and she's just now finding healing for the experience because we have a safe space to talk about it.

**David:** It's so easy to not think deeply enough about the words that come out of our mouths in the pulpit, to not contemplate who is in this audience, who is listening to me. Even at the grocery store, when we're talking with anyone, anytime words come out of our mouth in this realm, they need to be redemptive. Because we never know the stories of who we're talking with.

**Stacey:** I grew up in the church as a pastor's kid, being in church every Sunday and every Wednesday. I remember experiencing young women and teenagers who were facing unintended pregnancies and were not treated with love, compassion, or grace. So when I was facing an unintended pregnancy, I felt like I had to make the choice that I did because I didn't trust I would find grace in a faith community.

When you aren't able to be honest and vulnerable about what feel like the darkest parts of your story in a faith community, not only does that affect your relationships with others, but it ultimately affects your relationship with God. If I believe that my faith community will not hold my abortion story with grace and compassion, then how can I expect God to hold my abortion story with grace or compassion?

When you experience people in church having healthy, honest, transparent conversations about their struggles, failures, and all the things we normally try to hide, and those stories are held with grace and forgiveness, it completely changes your ability to worship in truth. It allows you to have deep relationships within your faith community, and it unlocks your ability to have an authentic relationship with God and to be fully known and loved by Him.

---

*Stacey and David live in the Midwest. They have been friends and part of the missionally oriented ministry David leads for nearly twenty years.*

# Conclusion

*God can do anything, you know—*
*far more than you could ever imagine or guess or request*
*in your wildest dreams! He does it not by pushing us around*
*but by working within us, his Spirit deeply and gently within us.*
*Glory to God in the church!*
*Glory to God in the Messiah, in Jesus!*
*Glory down all the generations!*
*Glory through all millennia! Oh, yes!*

EPHESIANS 3:20-21 MSG

IN THE PAST, WHEN I HEARD THIS VISION of God being able to do more than we can ever imagine, guess, or request, I tended to picture him doing something visible, instantaneous, and apart from me. So it takes me by surprise to hear that he does this by working "deeply and gently within us." It brings such a sense of peace and relief, because that is what I really want—deep and gentle change in myself and my fellow believers that goes beyond what I can imagine in our current divisive environment.

When we respond to the invitation to become more like Jesus, we open ourselves up to a whole new realm of possibilities. We are inviting the Spirit to work within us and overflow through us, and we can have faith that he will bring about more beautiful realities than we can even imagine.

Over and over, I am amazed by the people around me who are gently expanding the conversation with others in their spheres of influence by allowing God to transform them first. That is the beauty of growth in the kingdom of God. We dream big based on what God can do, and then start right where we are, which is all we can do. And we get to start right now.

# Acknowledgments

Dear Reader, I wrote this book hoping you'd find it. Thank you for exploring a prograce approach—your openness means more than you know.

To the guest essayists: Your stories paint a tangible picture of what is possible when we are united in radical grace. Thank you!

Thanks to the InterVarsity Press team: Kelli Trujillo for your commitment to the project and for treating it with such prayerful nuance; Al Hsu for your theological questions; and Karen Bonnell for your sensitive and thorough copyediting.

Thank you, Sarabeth Weszely Thorson, for drawing out the core message and editing my thoughts to express exactly what I wanted to say.

This book reflects two decades of countless conversations. While I cannot name everyone, I am deeply thankful for each person who has engaged with me and shaped my perspective.

Thank you to the ProGrace team—Katie Potts, Christy Singleton, and Selah Hirsch—for your unwavering commitment and for never complaining when my head was in the clouds!

To our ProGrace governing board—Jane May, Gwenn Garmon, Rev. Dr. Darice Wright, Jenna Gyorfi, and Rev. David Bisgrove—thank you for your constant support, wise leadership, and encouragement. I couldn't do this work without you. Thank you to our advisory board—Rev. Dr. Amy Peeler, Skye Jethani, and Kurt Tillman—your advice, ideas, and networking have been foundational. Thanks to Amy Peeler and David Bisgrove for your insightful theological feedback.

Thank you to the ProGrace supporter community for your generous investment into the church's potential—it makes this work a reality. To our Discover participants and Equip members, thank you for spreading this message throughout your sphere of influence. Thank you, Tammy Abernethy and Chris Whitford, for being early partners, encouraging friends, and spearheading the work in your cities.

Thank you to Denise Stein and the initial ProGrace board for sharing the vision and launching the organization with me. Also, thank you to all the board members and staff who have been part of these startup years, it has been a team effort.

To the community, board, and staff team around the Chicago pregnancy organization: Thank you for stewarding the vision ignited during those years. Through all the growth I also made many mistakes, and you extended much grace. I am grateful.

Thank you to Angie for starting that first support group, Willow Creek for saying yes, and Kim for walking alongside the women. That beautiful spark ignited my passion for who and what the church could be. Thank you to all the Chicago pastors and churches who piloted our workshop and support groups for women.

To Lacey Mason and Daryl Travis, thank you for the research that opened my eyes. To all the women who participated in the study, thank you for sharing your stories with clarity and vulnerability. Your voices are vital to this work.

Thank you, Laura McAlpine, for risking the relationship with Denise and me and introducing us to many others. I am also profoundly grateful to all those health professionals willing to share their honest opinions of our organization.

To everyone over the past twenty years who had the courage to disclose their experiences, frustrations, and disappointments with how Christians engaged with abortion, thank you. The cumulative effect of every conversation still impacts me and remains a core motivation for my work today.

To my friends and family: Thank you to the OG Redbud Writers Guild (and to Suanne Camfield for inviting me) for daring me to dream about this project.

To Christy Vines and Anne Snyder, thank you for being fellow dreamers and helping me feel normal.

To my friends who have listened to me process my passion about this issue countless times—Allison Reid, Barb White, Vicki Tysseling-Mattiace, and Jess Sales—thank you! Thank you to Cindy Nicholson and my Saturday morning group for faithfully praying for me.

Thank you to my mom, Joy Cramer Danzer, and my in-laws, John and Lorraine Weszely, for always supporting me and praying for me in whatever dream I decided to pursue.

Bob, I can't thank you enough for recognizing God's involvement when we first saw that positive pregnancy test. And for journeying with me to embrace a completely different approach to parenting and marriage. Sarabeth and Noah, I'm so grateful you showed me the craziness of trying to be a perfect mom. You both have shown remarkable maturity, connectedness, and humor as you helped me understand it's all about grace. Jesse, I'm grateful you jumped right into the chaos and openness of our family. I love you all so much!

# Notes

## INTRODUCTION

[1] Lisa Cannon Green, "Women Distrust Church on Abortion," Lifeway Research, November 23, 2015, https://research.lifeway.com/2015/11/23/women-distrust-church-on-abortion/.

[2] Aaron Earls, "7 in 10 Women Who Have Had an Abortion Identify as a Christian," Lifeway Research, December 3, 2021, https://research.lifeway.com/2021/12/03/7-in-10-women-who-have-had-an-abortion-identify-as-a-christian/.

## 2. TRANSFORMED BY GRACE

[1] "Brené Brown: Focus on Guilt Instead of Shame," *60 Minutes*, accessed April 4, 2024, https://youtu.be/RSrXxqKfYwI?si=329JrpnaCDj_rrl0.

[2] Mark Woods, "Bible Q&A: What Did Jesus Write in the Sand?," August 28, 2019, www.biblesociety.org.uk/explore-the-bible/bible-articles/bible-qa-what-did-jesus-write-in-the-sand.

[3] Lisa Cannon Green, "Women Distrust Church on Abortion," Lifeway Research, November 23, 2015, https://research.lifeway.com/2015/11/23/women-distrust-church-on-abortion/; CareNet, "Study of Women Who Have Had an Abortion and Their Views on Church," Lifeway Research, accessed April 4, 2025, https://research.lifeway.com/wp-content/uploads/2015/11/Care-Net-Final-Presentation-Report-Revised.pdf.

## 3. GRACE AND TRUTH ARE NOT CONTRADICTORY

[1] CareNet, "Study of Women Who Have Had an Abortion and Their Views on Church," Lifeway Research, accessed April 4, 2025, https://research.lifeway.com/wp-content/uploads/2015/11/Care-Net-Final-Presentation-Report-Revised.pdf.

## 4. TRANSCENDING PARTISAN POLITICS

[1] "Dobbs v. Jackson Women's Health Organization," National Constitution Center, accessed April 8, 2025, https://constitutioncenter.org/the-constitution/supreme-court-case-library/dobbs-v-jackson-womens-health-organization.

[2] Jeff Diamant, Besheer Mohamed, and Rebecca Leppert, "What the Data Says About Abortion in the U.S.," Pew Research Center, March 25, 2024, https://pewrsr.ch/3TRbxDV.

[3]Lee M. Jefferson, "The Healing Christ in Pandemics: Then and Now," *Interpretation* 77, no. 3 (July 2023): 233-45, https://pmc.ncbi.nlm.nih.gov/articles/PMC10265275/.

[4]Lydia Saad, "Historically Low Faith in U.S. Institutions Continues," Gallup, July 6, 2023, https://news.gallup.com/poll/508169/historically-low-faith-institutions-continues.aspx.

[5]Aaron Earls, "Public Trust in Pastors Falls to Historic Low," Lifeway Research, January 30, 2023, https://research.lifeway.com/2023/01/30/public-trust-in-pastors-falls-to-historic-low/.

[6]Lisa Cannon Green, "Women Distrust Church on Abortion," Lifeway Research, November 23, 2015, https://research.lifeway.com/2015/11/23/women-distrust-church-on-abortion/.

[7]Aaron Earls, "7 in 10 Women Who Have Had an Abortion Identify as a Christian," Lifeway Research, December 3, 2021, https://research.lifeway.com/2021/12/03/7-in-10-women-who-have-had-an-abortion-identify-as-a-christian/.

[8]Ryan Burge, "Religion in 2024: The Plateau Is Real," Graphs About Religion, April 7, 2025, www.graphsaboutreligion.com/p/religion-in-2024-the-plateau-is-real.

[9]Ryan Burge, "Gen Z and Religion in 2022," Religion in Public, April 3, 2023, https://religioninpublic.blog/2023/04/03/gen-z-and-religion-in-2022/.

[10]"Decline of Christianity in the U.S. Has Slowed, May Have Leveled Off," Pew Research Center, February 26, 2025, www.pewresearch.org/wp-content/uploads/sites/20/2025/02/PR_2025.02.26_religious-landscape-study_report.pdf.

[11]Ryan Burge, "Women Are More Religious Than Men, Right?," Graphs About Religion, June 19, 2023, www.graphsaboutreligion.com/p/women-are-more-religious-than-men.

[12]Michael Reneau, Matthew Loftus, and Evan Spear, "Quick Questions with Ryan Burge," *The Dispatch*, June 30, 2025, https://thedispatch.com/newsletter/dispatch-faith/africa-brain-drain-missionaries-christians/.

## 5. LISTENING TO WOMEN

[1]"One in Four US Women Expected to Have an Abortion in Their Lifetime," Guttmacher, April 17, 2024, www.guttmacher.org/news-release/2024/one-four-us-women-expected-have-abortion-their-lifetime.

[2]Isabel V. Sawhill and Kai Smith, "Abortion in the US: What You Need to Know," Brookings, May 29, 2024, www.brookings.edu/articles/abortion-in-the-us-what-you-need-to-know/.

[3]"Unintended Pregnancy," CDC Reproductive Health, May 15, 2024, www.cdc.gov/reproductive-health/hcp/unintended-pregnancy/index.html.

[4]Jeff Diamant, Besheer Mohamed, and Rebecca Leppert, "What the Data Says About Abortion in the U.S.," *Pew Research Center*, March 25, 2024, https://pewrsr.ch/3TRbxDV.

[5]Usha Ranji, Karen Diep, Bryana Castillo Sanchez, and Alina Salganicoff, *Key Facts on Abortion in the United States*, Women's Health Policy, KFF, July 15, 2025, www.kff.org/womens-health-policy/issue-brief/key-facts-on-abortion-in-the-united-states/.

[6]M. A. Biggs, H. Gould and D. G. Foster, "Understanding Why Women Seek Abortions in the US," *BMC Women's Health* 13 (July 2013): 29, www.ncbi.nlm.nih.gov/pmc/articles/PMC3729671/.

[7]"Emotional Inquiry," Brandtrust, accessed April 8, 2025, brandtrust.com/wp-content/uploads/2021/06/Emotional-Inquiry-Whitepaper.pdf.

## 6. RESISTING FALSE ASSUMPTIONS

[1]Margot Sanger-Katz, Claire Cain Miller, and Quoctrung Bui, "Who Gets Abortions in America?," *New York Times*, December 14, 2021, www.nytimes.com/interactive/2021/12/14/upshot/who-gets-abortions-in-america.html.

[2]Kenny & Associates, Inc, "Abortion: The Least of Three Evils," The Vitae Society, August 1994, www.heartbeatinternational.org/pdf/abortion-least_of_three.pdf.

[3]Liza Fuentes, Megan L. Kavanaugh, Lori F. Frohwirth, et al., "'Adoption Is Just Not For Me': How Abortion Patients in Michigan and New Mexico Factor Adoption into Their Pregnancy Outcome Decisions," *Contraception: X*, 5 (2023), www.sciencedirect.com/science/article/pii/S2590151623000023.

## 7. COLLECTIVE VERSUS INDIVIDUAL RESPONSIBILITY

[1]"Historical Development," SSA.gov, accessed August 4, 2025, www.ssa.gov/history/pdf/histdev.pdf.

[2]K. Kortsmit, M. G. Mandel, J. A. Reeves, et al., "Abortion Surveillance—United States 2019," *Morbidity and Mortality Weekly Report*, CDC, November 26, 2021, www.cdc.gov/mmwr/volumes/70/ss/ss7009a1.htm#T8_down.

[3]Maria Manansala, "Moms' Equal Pay Day Spotlight: Single Mothers, Poverty, and the Wage Gap," National Partnership for Women and Families, August 15, 2023, https://nationalpartnership.org/moms-equal-pay-day-spotlight-single-mothers-poverty-wage-gap.

[4]"The Childcare Cost Burden for Low-Income Households Around the US," United Way, October 14, 2023, https://unitedwaynca.org/blog/childcare-cost-burden-for-low-income-households-in-the-us/.

[5]"Childcare Costs, Reduced Work, and Financial Strain: New Estimates for Low-Income Families," June 27, 2024, US Dept. of Commerce, www.commerce.gov /news/blog/2024/06/childcare-costs-reduced-work-and-financial-strain-new -estimates-low-income.

[6]Cecilia Nowell, "New Mexico Made Childcare Free. It Lifted 120,000 People Above the Poverty Line," *The Guardian*, April 11, 2025, www.theguardian.com /us-news/2025/apr/11/childcare-new-mexico-poverty.

[7]Arthur Kellermann, "The U.S. Spends More on Healthcare Than Other Wealthy Nations but Ranks Last in Outcomes," Forbes, October 24, 2023, www.forbes .com/sites/arthurkellermann/2023/10/24/the-us-spends-more-on-healthcare -than-other-wealthy-nations-but-ranks-last-in-outcomes/.

[8]"Healthcare Is Least Affordable for Single Parents," CT Healthcare Affordability Index, accessed April 16, 2025, https://portal.ct.gov/-/media/ohs/ct-healthcare -affordability-index/chai/healthcare-affordabillity-and-single-parents-factsheet .pdf.

## 8. LOOKING BACK TO MOVE FORWARD

[1]"A Brief History of Pregnancy Resource Centers," ERLC, January 28, 2022, https:// erlc.com/resource/a-brief-history-of-pregnancy-resource-centers/; Margaret H. Hartshorn, "The History of Pregnancy Help Centers in the United States," Heartbeat International, March 13, 2007, www.heartbeatinternational.org/pdf /History_of_Centers.pdf; Dawn Stacey, "The Pregnancy Center Movement: History of Crisis Pregnancy Centers," Mother Jones, accessed April 17, 2025, https:// motherjones.com/wp-content/uploads/cpchistory2.pdf.

[2]Amy G. Bryant and Jonas J. Swartz, "Why Crisis Pregnancy Centers Are Legal but Unethical," *AMA Journal of Ethics*, March 2018, https://journalofethics.ama -assn.org/article/why-crisis-pregnancy-centers-are-legal-unethical/2018-03.

## 9. REFRAMING MOTHERHOOD

[1]Planned Parenthood v. Casey, 505 U.S. 833 (1992), accessed June 10, 2025, https://tile .loc.gov/storage-services/service/ll/usrep/usrep505/usrep505833/usrep505833.pdf.

[2]Whole Woman's Health v. Hellerstedt, 579 U.S. 582 (2016), accessed June 10, 2025, www.scotusblog.com/wp-content/uploads/2016/01/Janice-Macavoy-Paul -Weiss.pdf.

[3]Amalia R. Miller, "The Effects of Motherhood Timing on Career Path," *Journal of Population Economics* 24, (December 2009): 1071-1100, https://link.springer .com/article/10.1007/s00148-009-0296-x.

[4]Wei-hsin Yu and Yuko Hara, "Motherhood Penalties and Fatherhood Premiums: Effects of Parenthood on Earnings Growth Within and Across Firms," *Demography*,

February 12, 2021, https://read.dukeupress.edu/demography/article/58/1/247/167586/Motherhood-Penalties-and-Fatherhood-Premiums.

[5]K. Chin, A. Wendt, I. M. Bennett, and A. Bhat, "Suicide and Maternal Mortality," *Current Psychiatry Reports* 24, no. 4 (2022): 239-75, https://doi.org/10.1007/s11920-022-01334-3.

[6]K. Mangla, M. C. Hoffman, C. Trumpff, et al., "Maternal Self-Harm Deaths: An Unrecognized and Preventable Outcome," *American Journal of Obstetrics & Gynecology* 221, no. 4 (October 2019): 295-303, www.ajog.org/article/S0002-9378(19)30435-1/abstract.

[7]"Working Together to Reduce Black Maternal Mortality," CDC Women's Health, April 8, 2024, www.cdc.gov/womens-health/features/maternal-mortality.html.

[8]A. Njoku, M. Evans, L. Nimo-Sefah, and J. Bailey, "Listen to the Whispers Before They Become Screams: Addressing Black Maternal Morbidity and Mortality in the United States," *Healthcare* 11, no. 3 (February 3, 2023): 438, www.ncbi.nlm.nih.gov/pmc/articles/PMC9914526/.

[9]Nandita Bose, "Roe v Wade Ruling Disproportionately Hurts Black Women, Experts Say," Reuters, June 27, 2022, www.reuters.com/world/us/roe-v-wade-ruling-disproportionately-hurts-black-women-experts-say-2022-06-27/.

[10]Laura Ungar, "Scientists Show How Pregnancy Changes the Brain in Innumerable Ways," AP, September 16, 2024, https://apnews.com/article/pregnancy-brain-changes-mri-164b505abd05d3e5c9d93c0ef2953a80; L. Pritschet, C. M. Taylor, D. Cossio, et al., "Neuroanatomical Changes Observed over the Course of a Human Pregnancy," *Nature Neuroscience* 27, no. 11 (November 2024): 2253-60, https://pubmed.ncbi.nlm.nih.gov/39284962/.

## 10. REFORMING SEXUAL MYTHS

[1]Bob Smietana, "Willow Creek Elders and Pastor Heather Larson Resign over Bill Hybels," *Christianity Today*, August 8, 2018, www.christianitytoday.com/2018/08/willow-creek-bill-hybels-heather-larson-elders-resign-inves/.

[2]Daniel Silliman and Kate Shellnutt, "Ravi Zacharias Hid Hundreds of Pictures of Women, Abuse During Massages, and a Rape Allegation," *Christianity Today*, February 11, 2021, www.christianitytoday.com/2021/02/ravi-zacharias-rzim-investigation-sexual-abuse-sexting-rape/; Bob Smietana, "Report: Ravi Zacharias Was Guilty of Sexual Misconduct. RZIM Board Apologizes," *Religion News*, February 11, 2021, https://religionnews.com/2021/02/11/ravi-zacharias-report-massage-bangkok-selfies-masturbate-rzim-apology/.

[3]Kathryn Post and Bob Smietana, "Report Details 17 Cases of Abuse by IHOPKC Founder Mike Bickle," *Religion News*, February 5, 2025, https://religionnews

.com/2025/02/05/report-details-17-cases-of-abuse-by-mike-bickle-ihopkc
-founder/.

[4]Julie Roys, "Alleged Victim of Bill Hybels Tells Story of How Church Tried to
Silence Her," The Roys Report, February 28, 2020, https://julieroys.com/alleged
-victim-of-bill-hybels-tells-story-of-how-church-tried-to-silence-her/.

[5]"Open Letter from the International Board of Directors of RZIM on the Inves-
tigation of Ravi Zacharias," Anglican Link, February 12, 2021, https://anglican
.ink/2021/02/12/open-letter-from-the-international-board-of-directors-of-rzim
-on-the-investigation-of-ravi-zacharias/.

[6]Jaclyn Diaz, "The Scandal Roiling One of the Nation's Biggest Megachurches,
Explained," NPR, June 27, 2024, www.npr.org/2024/06/24/nx-s1-5017881
/robert-morris-gateway-church-sex-abuse-scandal-explained.

[7]Beth Moore, "A Letter to My Brothers," Living Proof Ministries Blog, May 3,
2018, https://blog.lproof.org/2018/05/a-letter-to-my-brothers.html.

[8]Halee Gray Scott, "Sexed-Up Culture Ruined Healthy Male-Female Work Relationships," *Christianity Today*, May 29, 2015, www.christianitytoday.com/ct/2015
/may-web-only/sexed-up-culture-ruined-healthy-male-female-relationships
.html; Halee Gray, "Let's Talk About Sex (and Ministry)," Biola University
YouTube, June 17, 2015, www.youtube.com/watch?v=HNjbwsfnLoQ.

[9]Daniel A. Cox and Kelsey Eyre Hammond, "Young Women Are Leaving Church
in Unprecedented Numbers," Survey Center on American Life, April 4, 2024,
www.americansurveycenter.org/newsletter/young-women-are-leaving-church
-in-unprecedented-numbers/.

[10]Ryan Burge, "We Asked the Nones a Bunch of Questions About Leaving Religion," July 15, 2024, Graphs About Religion, www.graphsaboutreligion.com/p
/we-asked-the-nones-a-bunch-of-questions.

[11]Rebecca Hopkins and Julie Roys, "Exclusive: 3rd Woman Says Mike Bickle
Groomed and Sexually Abused Her, Beginning at Age 15," The Roys Report, February 10, 2024, https://julieroys.com/third-woman-says-mike-bickle-groomed
-sexually-abused-her-beginning-at-age-15/; Mike Hixenbaugh and Antonia
Hylton, "Lawyer for Megachurch Pastor Blamed 12-Year-Old for Initiating 'Inappropriate' Sexual Conduct," July 9, 2024, NBC, News,www.nbcnews.com
/news/us-news/robert-morris-gateway-church-lawyer-letters-cindy-clemishire
-rcna160661.

## 11. REFRAMING WOMEN'S EQUALITY

[1]Caryn A. Reeder, *The Samaritan Woman's Story* (InterVarsity Press, 2022), 105.

[2]Jennifer Powell McNutt, *The Mary We Forgot* (Brazos Press, 2024), 23.

³Reeder, *The Samaritan Woman's Story*, 2.
⁴Powell McNutt, *The Mary We Forgot*.
⁵Ginny Lupka, personal interview with author.

## 12. A UNITED CHURCH

¹M. A. Biggs, H. Gould, and D. G. Foster, "Understanding Why Women Seek Abortions in the US," *BMC Women's Health* 13, 29 (2013), https://doi.org/10.1186/1472-6874-13-29.

## 13. CONVERSATIONS THAT CREATE COMMUNITY

¹"One in Four US Women Expected to Have an Abortion in Their Lifetime," Guttmacher, April 17, 2024, www.guttmacher.org/news-release/2024/one-four-us-women-expected-have-abortion-their-lifetime; "Unintended Pregnancy," CDC Reproductive Health, May 15, 2024, www.cdc.gov/reproductive-health/hcp/unintended-pregnancy/index.html.

# PRO*grace*®

Your journey of becoming more like Jesus in this conversation matters—and uniting with other believers around our shared Christian values matters more than our diverse political affiliations.

ProGrace supports Christians across all denominations in a new way of approaching abortion—grounded in theology, fueled by grace, and free from political division.

We invite you to continue this work, discovering resources and learning more at **prograce.org**.